T0204377

My Mentor

BOOKS BY
ALEC WILKINSON

....

MIDNIGHTS (1982)

MOONSHINE (1985)

BIG SUGAR (1989)

THE RIVERKEEPER (1991)

A VIOLENT ACT (1993)

MY MENTOR (2002)

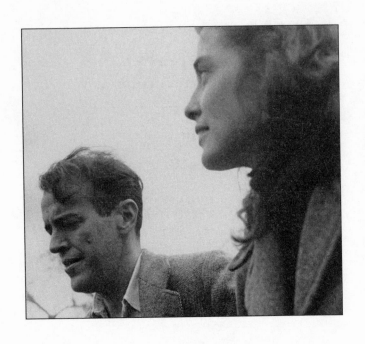

My Mentor

A Young Man's Friendship

with

William Maxwell

Alec Wilkinson

HOUGHTON MIFFLIN COMPANY

BOSTON · NEW YORK

2002

For information about permission to reproduce selections from
this book, write to Permissions, Houghton Mifflin Company,
215 Park Avenue South, New York, New York 10003.

Visit our Web site: www.houghtonmifflinbooks.com.

Library of Congress Cataloging-in-Publication Data

My mentor : a young man's friendship with William
Maxwell / Alec Wilkinson, date

p.   cm.

ISBN 0-618-12301-6

1. Maxwell, William, 1908–   2. Wilkinson, Alec, 1952–
— Friends and associates. 3. Authors, American —
20th century — Biography. 4. Editor — United States —
Biography. 5. Mentoring of authors. I. Title.

PS3525.A9464 Z96 2002

813'.54—dc21 [B] 2001051882

Printed in the United States of America

Book design by Robert Overholtzer

QUM 10 9 8 7 6 5 4 3 2 1

The author is grateful to Brookie Maxwell for
permission to quote from the writings of William Maxwell.

Frontispiece: William and Emily Maxwell, 1947
Photograph by Kirk C. Wilkinson

For Sara and for Sam

ACKNOWLEDGMENTS

I am grateful to Robert Gottlieb, C. P. Crow, and Ann Goldstein; to Benjamin Cheever; to Daniel Menaker and Charles McGrath; to Andrew Wylie, Sarah Chalfant, Kathy Robbins and David Halpern; to Eric Chinski; and to David Remnick, who suggested that I write about William Maxwell.

Above all, I would like to express my regard for and thanks to Kate Maxwell and to Brookie Maxwell and to my brothers — Stephan, Kirk, and Leland.

This is an account of how I found, in my father's friend, the attentive and affectionate paternal figure my father felt reluctant to be. An alternative father, that is. Why my own father wasn't comfortable in the role is something we never discussed. I suspect that he was a more complicated figure than I ever understood. Moodier, less sure of himself, struggling in ways that a child can perceive only by means of intuition. And with an awareness that the knowledge he now has in hand is too unsettling to bear much examination.

William Maxwell taught me a trade, which happened to be writing, but it doesn't require much in the way of imagination to believe that it might have been any trade. Its elements apply to most pursuits I can think of: a close attention; a responsiveness to impulse; a seriousness of purpose; a gathering of resources toward an intention, however opaque; a regard for others; and a delight in unexpected results.

Most people are hardly remembered five years after they die, but I will remember him — his writing, his character, his example, his advice — as long as I live.

As for the *mot juste,* you are quite wrong. Style is a very simple matter; it is all rhythm. Once you get that, you can't use the wrong words. But on the other hand here am I sitting after half the morning, crammed with ideas, and visions, and so on, and can't dislodge them, for lack of the right rhythm. Now this is very profound, what rhythm is, and goes far deeper than words. A sight, an emotion, creates this wave in the mind, long before it makes words to fit it . . .

— VIRGINIA WOOLF,
in a letter to Vita Sackville-West, 1926

One

WHEN I WAS A CHILD, William Maxwell and his wife, Emily, lived down the road from my parents, and Maxwell was my father's closest friend. My father was the art director of the magazine *Woman's Day.* Three days a week, Maxwell edited fiction at *The New Yorker,* and on the other four days he wrote novels and stories. My father drove to the train station by the Hudson River in a jeep he bought for twenty-five dollars from a dealer in Army surplus. On the mornings when Maxwell also took the train, my father stopped at the end of Maxwell's driveway and pressed on the horn. They were so comfortable with each other that if they spoke at all during the ride it was about the furnace not working properly, or the poison ivy taking over a stone wall, or how to keep a water pipe in the basement from freezing, or whether a woman who lived up the road was as pretty as my father insisted she was. Their intimacy was of the kind that excluded other people; a man who sometimes rode with them once said dismissively, "They're like an old married couple." When my father's first wife sat up late sewing a ruffle around the edge of the bed my father was trying to sleep in, Maxwell used it in a story, and when my mother, standing in his flower garden, remarked, "Children and roses reflect their care," he used that, too.

My father was an amateur photographer, and he took the portrait of Maxwell on the dust jacket of a novel he published in the nineteen-forties. He read Maxwell's books and was proud of their inscriptions to him and my mother on the flyleafs, and he clipped their reviews and stuck them between the books' pages, but he wasn't literary. He was impatient and earthy and impulsive. He was indifferent to social conventions, and his opinions were bluntly expressed — I doubt whether Maxwell ever said anything pointed without considering its effect on the feelings of the person he was talking to. My father was also unhesitating in his friendship. If the phone rang and it was Maxwell saying that a storm had blown a tree across his driveway or that his car wouldn't start, my father would stop what he was doing, find a saw or a gas can, and head down the hill to the Maxwells' house. I was aware of Maxwell among my father's friends; he was quieter than the rest of them and his face tended to give away his feelings.

Maxwell and my father were introduced by a neighbor on a commuter train platform, before Maxwell was married and had a family. He lived by himself in a cottage that had been delivered to its acre of ground on a flatbed truck, and he grew roses, and my father and his first wife lived up the hill, in a house with a horse barn and horses. My father understood anything he could put his hands on. In his barn he had a room full of tools, and he was an accomplished carpenter. I can imagine him and Maxwell in a scene that Maxwell described to me. It is evening, and darkness has already fallen. Maxwell stands beside my father while he cuts on his jigsaw the façade for the dollhouse that Maxwell is building for his daughters at Christmas.

My father was robust, and Maxwell's frame was slight. My father spent hours on the weekends in the fields and the barn attending to chores, while Maxwell sat at his typewriter. He liked to write in his pajamas and bathrobe and not shave or put on his clothes until he was done for the day, usually around lunchtime, or whenever he thought that his judgment was no longer reliable. He felt unable to write when he was tired. If he accepted an invitation from a neighbor to dinner, he rose from the table in time to be in bed by ten-thirty, with the hostess sternly observing him.

My father was charming and blasphemous and subversive by nature, and Maxwell took pleasure in the way that he embraced life. Whereas Maxwell's emotions tended to show on his face, my father had a tendency to say whatever was on his mind. If the company he was among disappointed him, he looked for new company. Maxwell's nature was sedentary. He disliked change. He didn't especially care for new experiences or all that much for travel, which is unusual in a writer, but Maxwell was a profoundly original writer. Except when he was a young man and had the idea that he might find something to write about if he went to sea, he didn't feel obliged to look around in the world for material. He drew almost entirely for his writing on his childhood in a small town in central Illinois — the sky, the farmhouses, the shaded streets, the flat prairie land; his relatives and neighbors, including the ones in the cemetery he only heard talked about; the subjects he listened to the adults dispose of as he lay on the couch and pretended to be asleep.

Maxwell's dependence on my father was practical, and my father's dependence on Maxwell was emotional. He knew no one else like Maxwell — so receptive, so kind, so quick to respond to gestures of friendship. Maxwell's company was a comfort to him, and my father was affectionate with Maxwell in a way that I never saw him be with another man. On the other hand, I know of no other of his friends who offered the opportunity. It was possible with Maxwell because Maxwell was unafraid of emotion. What people felt is what drew his interest, and he was deeply sympathetic. The gentleness my father expressed in Maxwell's company was balanced, I think, by a feeling that he bore some responsibility for Maxwell's well-being as a householder, the way one farmer might feel toward another the kind of masculine affection that involves a deep acceptance of the other's nature while also being concerned that his friend didn't know enough to come in out of the rain.

I grew up with an awareness of Maxwell, his kindness, his eyes which were expressive of emotion and calm and love, the figure he cut, polished and unhurried and attractive. When he asked me a question he was interested in the answer and wasn't made impatient by the repetitions and false starts children specialize in.

The dependence that he and my father shared was eventually passed on to me. When I was twenty-four I decided that I would try to become a writer, because it was clear to me that my hopes of being a rock-and-roll star weren't going to fly. I thought that by being a writer I could make a lot of money without working very hard; then I could go back to being a musician. What I planned to write about was the year I spent as one of nine policemen in Wellfleet, Massachusetts, on Cape Cod.

I had become a policeman partly because I regarded myself as a failure, and when I read the advertisement for the position it occurred to me that I might still manage a future for myself if I was a policeman for a year and then went to law school. Also, in the manner of many young men, I thought that I was in need of an experience that was solemn and rigorous and maybe a little bit dangerous, too. I wanted to be in the company of men who knew when it was proper to speak and what to say, and when it was better to say nothing at all. Who carried themselves with an offhand physical well-being that I could only impersonate. Lady-killers. I meant to add myself to them and pay close attention.

In the winter of 1970, while I was in my first year of college, my father quit his job in New York, and he and my mother moved to the house in Wellfleet they had built twenty years earlier. They bought an art gallery, where my father showed his paintings and those of artists he knew, and my mother kept the books. Because I left college for a while to go to California and be a musician, I graduated in December of 1974. A few months later, I read on a sheet of the town's stationery, tacked to the bulletin board on Main Street, the announcement of the policeman's job. In those days, a person reached the police department, above the fire department garage, by means of a long outdoor staircase. When I went through the door with my résumé, one policeman was talking to another. He knew I was there, but he did not break off from his story.

"Guy had this gigantic house," he said. "He was probably, oh, seventy-five, seventy-six. Easily two hundred and fifty pounds. And stubby, not that tall. A fireplug. He knew he was going to die, had a bad heart, wasn't a secret, doctor had told him. He must have had a feeling about it, because what he does is, just before he dies, he decides to go upstairs, and he finds the smallest room he could find — just a cot, a window, and a bureau — and he sits down, takes off his shoes, opens the window, says his prayers, crosses himself, and keels over.

"It's the afternoon now and we get the call. Maid found him, or somebody. Go get him. It took us an hour and fifteen minutes to get him out of there. *We* pushed, *we* pulled, *we* tugged, *we* lifted. And there's three of us in there, mind you, plus the guy makes four, so you could barely stand, let alone move. August, and I ain't caught my breath *lately*. And right across the hall was a big master bedroom. He *could* have gone in there. Very thoughtless."

He turned to me then and said, "What can I do for you?"

I handed him my résumé and said that I wanted to be a policeman. Then I didn't know what else to do, so I held out my hand and he shook it and I left.

At my interview with the town's selectmen, I met the Chief. He was six feet tall, his face was fleshy and high-colored, and with his uniform he wore his policeman's hat. When he shifted in his chair, I could hear his holster creaking. One of the selectmen said, "This is Alec Wilkinson. He has a degree in music."

The Chief said, "Music, huh? That'll be a big help. You ought to fit right in on the department."

A few months later, I asked him why he had hired me, and he said, "Well, it happened like this: there was another fellow, and he was more similar to my way of thinking, but he was committed to a job somewhere else.

That left you and another fellow, and he was unaccept-able."

I went to work for the first time on a Saturday night at the end of May. The sergeant was waiting for me, with a patrolman named Paul Francis. We went into the Chief's office, which the sergeant used at night. In one of the drawers of the desk, he found a pair of pistols. He weighed them in his hands, then gave me one of them. It had a small patch of rust on the barrel. "I think this one jams," he said of the gun he held on to. Then, "Maybe it's that one. Let me see." He examined them again, then gave me the one he originally held back. It didn't occur to me to ask what kind of gun it was, but I eventually learned it was a .38. I asked another officer, because I noticed that everyone else's gun was much bigger than mine was and also shot flames.

The sergeant asked if I had ever fired such a gun before, and I said that I hadn't. Paul said he would take me out to the firing range, but I guess he forgot.

"Where's the safety?" I asked.

"No safety," the sergeant said.

"You mean it could just go off?"

"No," he said, giving me an estimating look. "I mean, if you *drop* it, I suppose it could go off."

I said I wouldn't drop it, and he said that would be a good start.

In a closet he found a gun belt for me and a holster and some bullets. Then he said, "All right, you're all set."

Paul and I went out to the police car. I was very excited. We drove along the inlet in back of the station and when we came to a stop sign, Paul turned his head to watch a car going past. "I'm always observing a vehicle going by," he said soberly. "You keep a mental notebook — the license plate, the color, the year, the condition, the type, the driver, the passengers, where it's heading, or where it's just come from. Anyone along the side of the road. You never know when you'll use it. Down in Provincetown they got murders. By Jesus, the guys that did it drove through this town sure as hell. They could have done it right here and *taken* them to P-town, for all we know." He began moving the car slowly forward. "So murder could have happened here," he said, "and we don't know about it."

All but one of the other policemen were a few years older than I was. Most of them had been soldiers, and one or two had been to a war. Most of them were raising children. When I tried imitating the assurance they carried themselves with, I felt certain the effort was apparent. Twenty-five years later, I see them for what they were — intelligent and honorable young men at the beginning of lives that changed so substantially that some of them might be said to have collapsed. Several of their marriages dissolved. The Chief was unjustly fired and became a long-haul trucker and was changing a flat tire one night by the side of the road in Florida when he was struck by a car and killed. Another of them took a job with the post office. Another worked twenty years and retired; another drew disability payments because he had high blood pressure and a tendency to overexcitement, and now he drives a school bus. He also drove the school bus the year I was a policeman. One Saturday afternoon in the middle of the winter he walked down the aisle of the Catholic church, in the center of town, with a girl who had been on his route. I happened to pass by in the police car as the church doors opened and they came out and stood on the steps, having their picture taken. About being a policeman he liked to announce, "Your business is our business, and our business is none of your goddam business." Another was a fundamentalist Christian who ran his own trucking and hauling business. He would work from midnight to eight and go home and have breakfast and then haul brush or construction trash all day. His favorite maxim was "It's a great life if you don't weaken," which I didn't think much of at the time, but over the years it has struck me as more and more apt. Paul, someone told me, went over to the religious side of life. He had always been interested in Zen Buddhism and read whatever he could find on the subject. He thought that if he were in a state of enlightenment, he would probably be a better policeman. One night in the police car he told me that if his marriage ever broke up (it did), he would go to Japan and live in a monastery. "I'd hate like hell to do it," he said. "I mean my ego would. I'd think, How are you going to live without all the material things that seem so important to you, but I know you can." The others I have lost touch with.

I realize now that I became a writer partly from a love of music, partly from a sense of deprivation and the impulse to recover things I felt I had lost or never had, partly because it seemed to offer a means of finding order in the world, partly because a solitary childhood had accustomed me to observation and to isolation as a habit of work, and partly because I had something to write about. Driving around Wellfleet in the middle of the night and seeing whose lights were on because they couldn't sleep, or who walked the floors of their houses from night fears and anxiety. Picking up drunks on their way home in winter after the bars had closed and delivering them to their doors and having them fail to recognize me the next day when I stood behind them in line at the post office. Observing who waited until their husbands were away dragging nets on boats whose lights you could sometimes find at night on the horizon before bringing their lovers home. Arriving at someone's house after a child had called because his mother and father were arguing and he was afraid that one of them might reach for a kitchen knife or the shotgun or the pistol in the closet. Standing beside the old man or woman who had died while watching television for comfort in the middle of the night and been found in the morning by a neighbor. Cutting down the beautiful young woman who had hanged herself from the rafter of her cottage on Christmas Eve. Watching the fishing fleet leave the harbor in a procession toward the horizon at dawn, or the snow fall into the ocean. Firing a shotgun for the first time, to see what it was like, into the sand on the beach in the darkness of a slack moon and having everything go blue around me. Sharing the company of eight other young men I looked up to who couldn't have been more different from me.

During the summer for several hours a night I walked up and down Main Street. This was a job that usually fell to the specials — the local men who were carpenters or members of the town highway crew or just friends of the Chief and were hired part-time to expand the department. The Chief decided that it would be a broadening experience for me, though. "You'll get knocked down a few times up there, I guess," is what he said. "One guy I remember, a special, had a terrible time. He was just about your size, maybe a little bigger. I guess a little bigger. Anyway, the kids walked all over him. Every time he came down on them — told them to move or something — they threw him in the bushes. *They* told us this; the guy never did. To this day I can't figure out why he kept coming back. I guess he just liked to walk up and down the street with the uniform on."

Every evening a group of teenagers in two or three cars pulled into the town's parking lot and took seats on the bench in front of town hall, like a sullen little flock coming to roost. They found people to buy them beer and hard liquor, which they drank from bottles in paper bags. One of them, a small, defiant, and cherubic boy with curly blond hair, used to wear blue jeans and a black T-shirt that had an obscenity printed on it in white letters and, beneath it, "I am not a tourist. I live here and I don't answer questions." The oldest ones were hands in the fishing fleet and were bigger than I was, and they could see that it made me uneasy to confront them. They delighted in taunting me. Once, after midnight, I was at one end of the street when I heard a car stop, a few hundred feet behind me. In a moment several high-pitched voices called, "Officer. Oh, *Officer*," and then the car took off. I ran up the street, and when I arrived in front of the two-cash-register grocery store I saw something that was like a vision. The kids had sprayed the picture window with lighter fluid and set a match to it, and what I saw were flames that appeared to be floating several feet above the ground, as if nothing were on fire but the air. In a few more seconds they were gone.

Because I was new and awkward and unreliable and had never been properly trained, I usually worked from midnight until eight in the morning. Over the winter I worked by myself from two o'clock on. Before the other patrolman went home, we parked the newer of the cruisers outside the trailer where the Chief and his wife lived, in the woods above the highway, so that he could drive it to work in the morning. From Paul and another officer, named Joe Hogan, I learned to occupy myself when I was working with someone else by playing spotlight tag: one cruiser hid and one was it, and you were tagged when the other driver shined his spotlight on you. I learned that when enough snow had fallen, I could race the police car nearly the length of the parking lot at

Newcomb Hollow and then apply the brakes and spin the wheel and turn the car in circles. I learned to wait by the Cumberland Farms for Clem Silva, who drove the Provincetown ambulance. When he made a night run to the hospital in Hyannis, he would stop afterward at the donut store and fill the back of the ambulance with the leftover donuts and distribute them to the policemen along his way home. I learned that sometimes I could drive the length of Route 6, the state road through town, seven miles, on the wrong side of the yellow line and not meet anyone. One night on the police radio I heard a dispatcher in another town call his cruiser and say, "Uh, EZ-7, you want to check a report of a car on its roof on Route 137."

The policeman in EZ-7 said, "Yeah, would that be an accident, or what?"

And the dispatcher said, "Unless he *drives* it that way, it is."

I loved driving the police car. I loved the sense of privilege it gave me, knowing that I could go anywhere I wanted to — down any private road, up any driveway, past any No Trespassing sign — and no one could tell me not to. I loved knowing my way around the interior — which switch turned on the roof lights and which disengaged the shotgun from its bracket. I loved having the lights and the siren going and driving as fast as I could and having people need to get out of my way. I loved being in it late at night when the town was quiet and peaceful and I felt like a big fish finning its way along the bottom of its home river. It was the only part of being a policeman that I never grew tired of, but I never got any good at it, either. Driving down a back road on my first night alone, I lost control of the car heading into a turn and torpedoed into the woods. Another time, on a sand road out by the ocean, I tried to drive under a tree limb and broke the lights on the roof. Another time, going faster than I should have down a different sand road, I hit an exposed root with one of the front wheels and cracked the ball joint, and the wheel caved in and the car would go forward only in a circle. Another time, in the parking lot of the post office, I was engaged in a reverie and I drove slowly into a cement retaining wall. For a long time the Chief forbade me to drive a car unless no one else was working.

During the winter from midnight to eight there wasn't really much for me to do. Turn the doorknobs on the town's businesses to make sure they were locked. Arrest drunk drivers. Accompany the school bus in the morning. When I couldn't think of anything else to occupy me, I sometimes found a place in the woods or down by the ocean and turned the radio all the way up so that I would hear the dispatcher if she called, and closed my eyes. The way the light came into the sky in the morning made me think of sediment settling in water until the water slowly turns clear again.

I did not read many books as a child, and I read only three or four in college. One of them was *The Godfather,* which I read because I had seen the movie. Another was *Look Homeward, Angel,* by Thomas Wolfe, from which I retained only the sentence "The night was a cool bowl of lilac darkness." I thought that if such an observation was writing, I couldn't be a writer. One regarded the world poetically, or one didn't.

I considered writing a book because when I told people the things that were happening to me as a policeman, they usually said, "You should write a book." I bought a tape recorder then, and every night by myself in the police car, when I should have been working, I tried to describe what was happening to me, which was that I was sitting in the police car talking into a tape recorder. I now think it's strange that it didn't occur to me to write down the things that were happening, but it didn't. When the year was over, I sat at my typewriter. Nothing I wrote sounded genuine or convincing or even as if it had happened. I bought a ticket to Europe and stayed six months making money as a musician, and one night I stayed at a house in Paris, and from a shelf in the guest bedroom I took down a copy of *Across the River and Into the Trees,* by Ernest Hemingway. When I got to the end, I thought, I can do that. What gave me confidence was that Ernest Hemingway wrote very short sentences without flowery images, and he performed no pirouettes on the page. I didn't know there was more to writing than that. I also didn't know that the book is probably Hemingway's worst novel. I went home to Wellfleet with the plan of visiting my family at Thanksgiving and collecting the wardrobe I would need to write with pencils in notebooks in cafés in Paris, preferably at night, or maybe late in the afternoon, when the light would be perfect. For my picture on the dust jacket I was pretty sure I would wear a beret. I also thought I would include a preface, which I would sign, *AW, Paris, France.*

I don't remember why I gave up the idea of going back to Paris, but I did. I sat down in a room again and resolved to get to work. When I had completed two chapters, I sent them to a writer my parents knew. He showed them to the editor who published his books, and she wrote back, saying, "I cannot encourage this young man enough to abandon this project."

I persevered by thinking that I was the only young person in America writing a book. At least I didn't know anyone else who was writing a book. Anyway, I was the only one writing a book about being a small-town policeman.

It was my father's idea that I show what I was writing to Maxwell. I wouldn't have thought of it on my own. I didn't know the regard that serious writers had for Maxwell's work and his opinions. I saw his name on the spines of his books on my parents' bookshelves, but I hadn't read the books. I read books quickly and promiscuously then and without much appreciation for what the writer was up to. I was protected by my innocence from feeling self-conscious about the writing that I was showing to Maxwell, and he was not the sort of person who felt the need to impress people, to have an audience or acolytes; there was nothing in him of the self-inflater. A few years earlier he had retired from *The New Yorker*, after forty years, and was devoting himself to writing, and except occasionally, when a friend showed him a draft of a novel, no one was asking for his help. The writers who sometimes dedicated their books to him and who had relied on his judgment — Salinger, Nabokov, Cheever, Welty, Updike, John O'Hara, Frank O'Connor, Shirley Hazzard, Sylvia Townsend Warner, Mavis Gallant, Larry Woiwode, Allan Gurganus, and Harold Brodkey among them — sent him what they had written in the hope that he would buy it, not that he would show them how to make it into something they might publish.

I'm sure that he never before saw writing as naïve as mine, unless it was during the period in his twenties when he taught writing to college freshmen. At *The New Yorker* a story in so unpromising a state wouldn't have come to his attention; someone would have seen it first and rejected it. What he saw that made him encourage me, I don't know. All he said was that I learned quickly, which must at least have made him feel that he wasn't wasting his time. Undoubtedly he was helping me because of his feelings for my father.

For the last ten years of Maxwell's life — he was ninety-one when he died, in the summer of 2000 — I tried to hold in mind the awareness that he wouldn't be here forever. He came close to dying on two occasions, from pneumonia, the old person's friend. The first time he got it, he misunderstood a doctor in the emergency room who asked whether he wished to have extraordinary measures taken to keep him alive. What he thought the doctor was asking was whether he wanted his life maintained by a machine if he had a collapse, and he didn't. The next morning he gave an account of things that had gone on in the intensive care ward during the night that couldn't possibly have happened, but in a few weeks he came home to his apartment on the Upper East Side and picked up his life again; that is to say, had people to tea, walked along the river, read, wrote.

His wife, whom he loved dearly, began a course of chemotherapy. In addition, a form of cancer he had suffered almost twenty years earlier appeared to be returning. He began to decline. I read his books again. I read letters I'd got from him. I talked to him almost every day on the phone, and I saw him as often as I could. He and his wife were no longer able to use the house in the country, the one on the road where I had grown up, and my wife and son and I went to it nearly every weekend. I worked at his desk. I watered the geraniums on the sill in his study. I wore his down jacket when I went for a walk. I wrote a piece about him for *The New Yorker*, and after it was published I decided that I wanted to write something more. Before I began, Mrs. Maxwell died, at seventy-eight, on July 23, 2000. Maxwell died eight days later. I wrote something to read at the memorial service Mrs. Maxwell planned with her daughters. Sometimes while I wrote, I felt tears prick the backs of my eyes and had to stop and brush them away. I was aware that Maxwell had wept while writing one of his novels that dealt with the death of his mother, and it made me feel as if I were imitating him, but I missed him so much that I didn't seem able to stop. Furthermore, I didn't care if I was imitating him. What difference would it make if I were.

The service was held on a mild afternoon in the fall at the Cathedral of St. John the Divine. Hundreds of people came. Afterward, as Mrs. Maxwell had specified, there was a horse to take the children on rides and ice cream for everyone. Even so, I found it a difficult experience. The formality of the occasion and its somber purpose insisted that I accept that they were gone, and I wasn't prepared to.

I had expected that when the memorial passed, I would return to writing about Maxwell. No other subject meant anything to me. To my surprise, I found I could write nothing about him except generalities. Years ago I had shown Maxwell a draft of a story I was trying to write about my mother that had come to a dead end. He read it and said, "Is that all you have to say about your mother?" I knew that there was a lot more that I wanted to say about Maxwell, but when I tried to write, I felt as if I couldn't remember what it was, or, when I could, that it didn't amount to much after all. It was as if I hadn't known him as well as I thought I had. I was grateful for Maxwell's friendship and influence. I knew that he didn't care to be grieved over, and that he had lived a long and happy life. "Who ever would have thought," he once said, "that the fragile little boy from Lincoln would have had such a time of it." And I knew that he had accomplished something very few writers in his century had: he had written books that lasted. But even so I felt an immobility that kept me from doing what I wanted to do.

I decided that it was one thing to write about Maxwell when he was alive, and, by writing, not only hope superstitiously to keep him alive but also to declare my feelings for him, and that it would be another to write about him if he had been dead for several years and I had had time to become reconciled. It was different, though, to write about him while I felt so bereft. It was probably not possible. I could not, apparently, make the portion of me that was resistant take part if it wasn't inclined to.

A few weeks after the service, I was awake in the middle of the night. After the Second World War, the Maxwells spent four months traveling in France, where Mrs. Maxwell had been as a child and Maxwell had never been. They intended to look for two things she remembered: a church at the end of a streetcar line, and a chateau with a green lawn in front of it. At the sight of the coastline through the porthole of their cabin, Maxwell felt a stirring in his heart that was wholly unexpected. Every town they saw, every street, every experience, even the weather and the brightness of the air, made an impression on him. They stayed until their money ran out. As I lay awake, I remembered his saying that when he walked in the door of the house in the country, before he took off his coat or his hat, he rolled a piece of paper into his typewriter and wrote down all the things that he hoped to include in a novel about an American couple making a tour of France. *The Chateau* took him more than ten years to write. It was his way, he said, of not coming home, of creating a facsimile of France in his imagination and inhabiting it. As I thought of this, something within me relaxed its grip, and I knew that when I sat down to work the next morning, I would be able to write.

To console, on the occasion of the death of her mother, the daughter of a young woman who had grown up with Mrs. Maxwell, Maxwell wrote to her, near the end of his life, "I see no reason to doubt that people have souls, and animals too, and what happens when the soul and the body part company, if they do, is anybody's guess, but over our hearts, death has no dominance."

This account of my friend and what he taught me is my means of refuting his death.

HAVING MY MOST INTIMATE friend be nearly twice my age did not seem unusual to me, partly because I am no longer captivated by things that younger people are concerned with. I attribute this to having been the youngest by far in a family of four brothers. Every privilege, every opportunity, every excitement and pleasure appeared to be reserved for people older than I was. When I arrived at a landmark I had seen on the horizon, my brothers had given it up for another that was just as remote. What was behind me didn't seem valuable. I also don't much care what younger people are interested in because I was young, and I remember what it was like. I have no desire to have the same experiences, or to re-enact them at second hand through the experiences of people who now are young. Popular culture tirelessly celebrates excess, outrage, and adolescent beauty, none of which appeals to me anymore. To have too close an interest in the lives of young people at this point in my life would amount nearly to a perversion. Further-more, it seems unnatural to me to be unwilling to get older. It takes courage, of course, but the pleasures only deepen, and the most fortunate of us achieve some sort of wisdom.

A few years ago, Knopf published a volume of letters exchanged by Maxwell and Frank O'Connor, the Irish writer whose real name was Michael O'Donovan. It is called *The Happiness of Getting It Down Right*. Maxwell describes being awakened at night by his daughters when they were little, or the difficulty he is having mak-ing a piece of writing come out, or a trip to his in-laws on the Oregon coast, and I read the letters closely be-cause, except for the material about his childhood that appears in his books or that he described in interviews, I knew hardly anything about his life when he was young. He was a figure from my childhood, and whatever daydreams I had then didn't include imagining what older people were doing when I didn't see them or who they might have been when they didn't look exactly as I was accustomed to having them look.

It is not my plan to write a literary biography. Someone else will do that; I haven't got either the objectivity or the critical equipment the project requires. If I am to persuade you, though, of why Maxwell meant so much to me, I have first to give an account of what he was like and a suggestion of what made him that way. Style is character. Over time we cannot help revealing ourselves to anyone who is paying close attention. It doesn't even require from them much in the way of a talent for awareness. What depth we might have, the complexity of our natures, our capacities for sympathy, and a mature relation to self-interest. Whether or not we can be trusted, not only with secrets but to regard another person's existence with the same importance we view our own with.

As briefly as I can, then, and before I take up the education he gave me, I would like to tell what I know of Maxwell's past and to describe him. When we are young, the world seems full of great men and women, and as we grow older we lose them. He was the greatest man I ever knew, and there will be, I hope, if I manage it accurately, some benefit — something sustaining and inspiring — in recalling him. The worst I can be, after all, is wrong.

Maxwell was an elderly man when his older brother died, and he realized, he told me, that "no one any longer remembers the things that I do," meaning the house in Lincoln, Illinois, where they lived with their mother and father, and which they left for an apartment in Chicago when their younger brother was two. Toward the end of his life it was borne in on me that if I didn't ask him about his past, there would be no one to enlighten me once he was gone.

He was born on August 16, 1908. As a child he heard horses pulling wagons up the street past his parents' house. Twelve thousand people lived in Lincoln, many of them farmers or coal miners or the descendants of such people. Maxwell's father was the species of traveling businessman called a drummer — someone whose responsibility, that is, was to drum up work for his company. He loved nothing more than being home. Here are some sentences about him from Maxwell's story "The Front and Back Parts of the House," written when he was in his eighties and his father had been dead for thirty years:

"Though it took me a while to realize it, I had a good father. He left the house early Tuesday morning carrying his leather grip, which was heavy with printed forms, and walked downtown to the railroad station. As the Illinois state agent for a small fire and windstorm insurance company he was expected to make his underwriting experience available to local agents in Freeport, Carbondale, Alton, Carthage, Dixon, Quincy, and so on, and to cultivate their friendship in the hope that they would give more business to his company. I believe he was well liked. Three nights out of every week he slept in godforsaken commercial hotels that overlooked the railroad tracks and when he turned over in the dark he heard the sound of the ceiling fan and railway cars being shunted. He knew the state of Illinois the way I knew our house and yard."

Maxwell's attachment to his mother was such that when some instinct told him that she was no longer in the room, he would often pick himself up and go looking for her. These sentences are from his novel *So Long, See You Tomorrow*, published in 1980:

"My younger brother was born on New Year's Day, at the height of the influenza epidemic of 1918. My mother died two days later of double pneumonia. The worst that could happen had happened, and the shine went out of everything. Disbelieving, we endured the wreath on the door, and the undertaker coming and going, the influx of food, the overpowering odor of white flowers, and all the rest of it, including the first of a series of housekeepers, who took care of the baby and sat in my mother's place at mealtime."

And: "My mother's sisters and my father's sisters and my grandmother all watched over us. If they hadn't, I don't know what would have become of us, in that sad house, where nothing ever changed, where life had come to a standstill. My father was all but undone by my mother's death. In the evening after supper he walked the floor and I walked with him, with my arm around his waist. I was ten years old. He would walk from the living room into the front hall, then, turning, past the grandfather's clock and on into the library, and from the library into the living room. Or he would walk from the library into the dining room and then into the living room by another doorway, and back to the front hall. Because he didn't say anything, I didn't either. I only tried to sense, as he was about to turn, which room he was going to next so we wouldn't bump into each other. His eyes were focused on things not in those rooms, and his face was the color of ashes."

Maxwell's father was handsome and fond of the company of women. He had three small children to take care of, and no one expected he would live out his life as a widower. Having observed a period of mourning that lasted several years, he remarried, and two years after that was promoted to a position that required him to move to Chicago. Maxwell wrote poetry in high school, and to illustrate posters for the drama society made pen-and-ink drawings in the style of Aubrey Beardsley. Answering a questionnaire for an academic when he was eighty-nine, Maxwell wrote that he didn't really think that he could say what were the most exciting moments of his career, there had been so many. Looking through a porthole at the age of forty and seeing the coast of France, the day his wife agreed to marry him, the days on which his two daughters were born, reading Tolstoy's

Master and Man for the first time. "Perhaps," he also wrote, "it was my meeting with the Wisconsin novelist Zona Gale when I was seventeen."

Maxwell had gone to Wisconsin for the summer with a friend who had talked a man there into giving him and Maxwell jobs at a lake near Portage. "The man who gave us the job had got drunk and agreed to it with my friend," Maxwell told me, "and when I showed up, I weighed a hundred and twelve pounds and was frail. They were dismayed, but I was stronger than I looked. My friend became a lifeguard, and I worked on cleaning out a basement, but there wasn't enough for me to do. There was a woman in the town named Mrs. Green, who was of an enthusiastic nature and took crushes on people, and she gave me a job on her farm, and the day I arrived, her older daughter said, 'I have some strawberries to give to Mr. Gale.' She took me with her, and while she was talking to Mr. Gale, who sat in a chair on the porch with a blanket over his knees, Zona showed me around the house. She was more than thirty years older than I was and soft-spoken, and we talked only about me, which at that age was something. She treated me as her intellectual equal, and I was by no means that. I had just finished my junior year of high school.

"The next day I was pulling weeds in the vegetable garden when I heard the phone ringing. A few minutes later Mrs. Green came out on the porch and said, 'That was Miss Gale. She said come to dinner Wednesday and bring the little Maxwell.' She was not quite of her time;

she was a mistake. No one much reads her now or even knows who she is, but in those days there was a good chance that if you picked up a magazine you might find a story of hers in it, and her play *Miss Lulu Bett* won the Pulitzer Prize. She wrote for ladies' magazines for money and then she wrote serious books, and sometimes the two got mixed up, especially toward the end of her life. She was absolutely angelic to me. She once wrote me a letter from Japan to say that after a dinner at which she had been the guest of honor, four hundred fireflies had been let loose in the garden for their amusement. Which was what any adolescent would like to hear, that life was not flat."

Maxwell planned to study painting at the Chicago Art Institute. What happened instead is that the friend he had gone to Wisconsin with came down with pleurisy while working as a lifeguard. The boy's parents thought his health wasn't good enough to allow him to attend the University of Illinois at Urbana, but Maxwell said he would help him do what was necessary, and his parents agreed. Maxwell liked the campus and enrolled. "If my friend hadn't got pleurisy," he said, "I would have enrolled, as I'd planned to do, in the Chicago Art Institute and perhaps not have been a writer at all but some hack artist, for I wasn't all that talented."

Maxwell graduated second in a class of twelve hundred. Among the honors he collected was a scholarship to graduate school offered by the Harvard Club of Chicago. In those days, a doctorate in English required a reading knowledge of German. Maxwell had taken two years of German as an undergraduate, but something happened to him over the summer so that when he got to Harvard all German words looked alike, including the prefixes and suffixes. Since he had had no trouble in college with Latin, French, Greek, or Italian, he assumed the difficulty was the result of the political cartoons he had seen as a boy in the pages of the Lincoln *Evening Herald* — Huns with babies spitted on their bayonets and Belgian women with their hands cut off. He thought that the textbooks' being printed in Gothic letters may have contributed to the problem.

To overcome his deficiency, Maxwell enrolled at Harvard in an advanced undergraduate course on the works of Goethe, which he memorized in English so that when they appeared on his graduate exams he could recognize them and remember what they were about. Day after day he set his alarm clock for five in the morning in order to have more hours to study. By February he was so tired that one morning when the alarm went off, he couldn't get out of bed. He lay in the dark with tears running down his face. Finally he summoned the memory of his father's father, who as a young man walked from Ohio to Illinois looking for a job teaching school. He died before Maxwell was born, but Maxwell asked for his help and felt that he got it. He ended up with a B in the course when a C would have been failing. With so undistinguished a showing, he couldn't expect further scholarship.

In the fall he went back to the University of Illinois and for two years taught writing to freshmen and graded papers for a course on Tennyson. That without a reading knowledge of German he would be unable to get a Ph.D. at Urbana or anywhere else and become a professor of English or even be allowed to go on indefinitely grading freshman papers was a fact that he somehow concealed from himself.

As is common in university towns, people with big old houses rented rooms to students. Maxwell lived in the house of a retired banker whose daughter, Garreta Busey, was a member of the English department. She had been on the staff of the New York *Herald Tribune* weekly book section. The paper sent her books to review and once, when there was a death in the Busey family, she turned the job over to Maxwell. After that, the paper sent books to both of them. "Garreta was several years older than I was," Maxwell told me, "and I have never had a better friend. She was strikingly beautiful, with her dark hair, braided, worn in a crown around her head. She was highly intelligent, humorous, witty, generous, and with literary aspirations of her own. She published a novel, *The Windbreak*, about Illinois farm life, and a volume of her poetry was published after she died."

A professor at Yale asked Busey to turn a two-volume life of Thomas Coke of Holkham into forty pages. Coke was an agriculturist of the late eighteenth century. Busey wrote about his farming innovations and gave Maxwell the parts that dealt with his social life, the parties and balls, and especially his aunt, Lady Mary Coke, who refused to live with her husband, who was boorish, dressed her servants in pea-green and silver, fished in her ornamental goldfish pond when she was melancholy, corresponded with Horace Walpole, suffered from the delusion that the Empress Maria Theresa was trying to hire away her servants, and in old age slept in a dresser drawer.

"All this gave me such delight," Maxwell said, "that when the job was done, I turned to and wrote a novel, so I could go on making sentences. Up to that time I had written poetry exclusively, but I was not actually a poet. Anyway, it didn't end there. I had a vision of the course of my life, through the various stages of advancement until I became a professor emeritus and was carried out in a wooden box. I didn't want to know what my life was like before I led it, so one day I went into the office of the chairman of the English department and resigned. In the year 1933, the worst period of the Depression, it would be hard to think of anything more foolhardy."

To finish his novel, which he first called *Snake-Feeders*, then *Thundercloud*, and finally *Bright Center of Heaven*, Maxwell moved to Mrs. Green's farm in Wisconsin and did work around the place in exchange for meals and a place to sleep. This is from a story, written when he was nearly ninety, called "The Room Outside":

"When I was in my middle twenties, I spent a winter on a farm in southern Wisconsin. There it was much colder than it was in Illinois, where, with the wind coming down from Lake Michigan, God knows it is cold enough. Bales of hay were banked all around the foundations of the farmhouse, which was heated by two sheet-iron wood-burning stoves, one upstairs and one downstairs in the room next to my small bedroom. And, of course, the cookstove in the kitchen. In the morning when I woke I sometimes saw a broad band of yellow light in the sky that I have never seen anywhere else, and before I could wash my face I often had to break a thin glaze of ice in the water pitcher on my dresser. The window had to be propped open, by a wooden spool in ordinary weather, a smaller spool if the temperature was twenty below, and if it was colder than that I didn't open the window at all. It was up to me to see that the wood-box in the kitchen was never empty and fill the reservoir on the side of the stove. The air was usually so dry you could run out of the house in your shirtsleeves and fill a bucket of water at the pump but you couldn't touch the pump handle with your bare hands. I also had to keep a patch of ground bare and sprinkled with corn for the quail. If it rained when the temperature was hovering around thirty-two degrees their feathers froze and they couldn't fly into the shelter of the woods.

"Eventually there was so much snow on the roads that the snowplow couldn't get through and we were snowbound. One evening after supper the telephone rang, and it was a neighbor saying that the mailman had got as far as the Four Corners, where our mailbox was. I put on extra-heavy underwear and, bundled to the eyes in sweaters and woolen scarves, I started to ski to the Four Corners. The snowdrifts were higher than the horse-and-rider fences, obliterating the divisions between the fields, and I saw what nobody in the family and none of the neighboring farmers had ever seen: a pack of wild dogs running in a circle in the bright moonlight."

When the book was done, he took it to Zona Gale and asked her not whether it was any good, but whether it was a novel. She said that it was. In late 1933, before it had been accepted by a publisher, Maxwell went to New York. On the dust jackets of the period the author had commonly been to sea, and Maxwell hoped that if he found a ship in the harbor that would take him aboard, it would give him something to write about. He was twenty-five years old. At a party he met a man who wrote popular sea stories and who gave him a letter of introduction to the captain of a four-masted schooner that belonged to J. P. Morgan and was anchored in Gravesend Bay, off Staten Island. Maxwell hired a row-boat to take him out to the ship, where he found that the man his letter was addressed to had left the day before. The only member of the crew was a sailor chipping rust, with a police dog beside him. The new captain read Maxwell's letter and then explained that the ship had not left anchor in four years and was not likely to. A family friend had also arranged an interview for Max-well at B. Altman's, a department store, where there was an opening for an elevator boy, but the personnel manager decided he was too well educated. "After a week," he said, "you'd be insulting the customers."

Maxwell was living in the Railroad Men's YMCA on Lexington Avenue at Forty-ninth Street, and in their library he came on a book by Lafcadio Hearn about the beautiful city of St. Pierre, Martinique. He decided to go there but discovered that it had been destroyed by a volcanic eruption in 1902. Even so, he thought, there must be vestiges of it still, and he booked passage on a small, dingy freighter, in February. The decks were covered with temporary stables to accommodate a cargo of Missouri mules. There were six passengers in the dining salon. One was a British novelist who dressed for dinner as if she were on the *Mauritania.* Two Y-shaped scars on her cheeks suggested an inept face-lift. She said she was a countess, and the crew were seen everywhere reading copies of her books. Maxwell was reading *War and Peace,* and she asked him if he was traveling incognito. In the end she overcame his snobbish resistance, and they became friends. He got off the boat at Trinidad and stayed there several days. On one of them he went to the races. In the evening, when they were over, immigrants from India set up card tables all around the track and gambled by candlelight.

From Trinidad he took a boat to Martinique, where the next morning there was a double rainbow over the harbor at Fort-de-France, and the purser gave him the name of a good *pension.* In an effort to gather material he wandered through the streets. The women wore the costume Hearn had described — a madras turban and a dress with a small bustle — but nothing else was recognizable. It was carnival time, and he was sometimes accosted by two or three towering young black men dressed in baby clothes, who demanded small sums of money. And there was a man with a lion's mane with little bells in it who roamed the streets with fifty little boys following him chanting antiphonally. The movies in the theaters he had already seen. The gray volcanic sand made the beaches uninviting. At nine o'clock the light went on in the kitchen of the *pension*, and at ten food began to appear on his table, in an open courtyard. It was better food than he had ever had anywhere. At midnight he drew the mosquito netting around him as he fell into bed, drunk from the wine in his carafe. In the crotches of the trees orchids bloomed, and sewage ran down the gutters. He sometimes stood in the door of a dance hall. The music consisted of a single phrase repeated endlessly. The dancers, without moving their feet, ground their pelvises together. The book he had hoped to write eluded him. He sat on a bluff looking out to sea. For the first time in his life he was homesick. A month in Martinique, where he went days at a time without speaking to anyone, seemed like a year in America. One night when he sat down to dinner he found a letter telling him that Harper and Brothers was seriously considering publishing his novel, and he went back on the same freighter he had arrived on.

When the novel appeared, Maxwell was hoping the newspapers would carry large ads. On the day of publication, the publicity director took him to lunch and said, "Now we must pray." The reviews said "promising," and the first edition of a thousand copies sold out, the second didn't, and it is now a collector's item. The central character is a flighty woman who, in the incessant pursuit of order, induces disorder instead. She is reduced to taking paying guests, and when she invites a distinguished black man for the weekend it is more than the social fabric can bear, and there is a partly comic and unmanageable situation. Maxwell never allowed it to be republished.

From photographs kept in a cabinet in the study of the Maxwells' house in the country, I know that as a boy his features were so finely drawn that he looked almost like a girl. As a young man he had a narrow face, full lips, and a wide, thin mouth. He had brown hair, and his eyes were dark and watery and expressive to the point of radiance, and they remained so all his life. At parties, which he wasn't especially fond of, he tended to find one person whom he could talk to. His voice was whispery, and in order to be heard he sometimes drew a breath and paused or hunched his shoulders and leaned forward. The remarks he made in a tone of voice slightly clearer than his usual one were things you knew he felt strongly about. His posture was slightly stooped from years of sitting at the typewriter. He was about five feet eight inches tall and so slender as to be nearly delicate. His skin toward the end of his life was like paper. His health was always robust, and he had surprising strength, but he was never an athlete.

When you looked into his eyes you felt you were looking into the eyes of someone who understood and accepted you. And didn't require from you something more than you could provide. Or that you be anyone but yourself. Unlike my father's, his attention was not restless. His acceptance made you feel valued. His friends often felt that no matter what they did, he was unlikely to view their behavior judgmentally. It is not that he was without opinions concerning right conduct, or that his moral standards were elastic; it is that once he regarded someone as a friend, he was likely to consider his or her actions sympathetically, as a response to the complications of life or as understandable within the context. He was aware that people don't always act in their best interests, and often make choices that appear to work against them. Self-destructive behavior has its allure and is not easily resisted. When he was in college and distraught over the loss of his closest friend, he cut his wrists with a razor; the event is the climax of *The Folded Leaf*. So far as I know, it is the only act of violence he ever committed.

In his thirties he lived in the country with an elderly French housekeeper. When a neighbor asked about him she said, "He reads, he writes. He writes, he reads." Something in her tone conveyed a mild disapproval. He had read everything worth reading and knew the value of it, and was unmoved by the accepted wisdom or pieties. He was fiercely literate and yet never made a show about it — he had none of the complacency of the academic, and nothing of the critic. That is, he did not try to understand writing by means of the history of the writer, or from what other people said about the writer, or the circumstances of the writer's social life, or whether he had honored certain conventions, or the impression he made at a dinner party, or his appearance in photographs; he knew instead whether the writer had managed what he was attempting in a manner that was dramatic and consistent with the weight of his material and was brilliant or not, or was overwritten, or thought into being rather than felt. Writing that is brought into being by means of thought — that is, writing that draws on what a writer has read and absorbed and has not changed or affected him but made him feel he has capital to spend on advancing himself, that is done without the engagement of the emotions, or in imitation of writing that has been done before, or that is secondhand, or that observes customs — left him unmoved, no matter how popular it might be. The writer's name on a story, known or not, had no influence on his opinion. The writing engaged him or it didn't. His judgment was acute and penetrating. This is from a letter written when he was in middle age, during the sixties: "Perhaps if I read the poems that are being published in *The New Yorker* just now more conscientiously I would enjoy them, but I tend not to, and I have just begun to see why. They seem as often to be concerned with unconscious rather than conscious feelings, and unconscious feelings can only be expressed, it would appear, by a display of virtuosity in arranging objects and disconnected glimpses of experience." Far better writers than I thought his estimation was unfailingly reliable.

He was sometimes difficult to talk to, because he had no interest in facile or socially polite conversation, lunch party talk. His conversation was about things that mattered to him, and he was not made uncomfortable by hesitations or breaks in an exchange. His silences appeared to be measuring and sometimes made me anxious. It was years before I understood that his habit was to brood until he felt moved to respond. No one's conversation was more literate or informed or compressed. His remarks had the candor and perception and quality of profound thought. Often he said no more than a sentence. In general, as people get older they talk more and become insensitive. As Maxwell got older he talked less and listened more, a form of kindness and an expression of his never-ending interest in the world.

Many of his observations were succinct and subtle and inherently dramatic. As an elderly man, he was driving once in a heavy rain. The turn he made — near the top of a hill, across a lane of traffic onto a road that led to the one where he and his wife lived — was tricky, even in good weather. The car whose path he turned into he never saw. At eighty-seven he walked away from a head-on car crash. The other driver turned out to be a fortune hunter. Deposing Maxwell, the driver's lawyer asked, "How long did the accident take?" Maxwell said, "I thought to myself, you must accept whatever happens." The lawyer complained that it was pointless talking to Maxwell; he clearly didn't understand the questions. His mind was not elegant enough to apprehend that Maxwell had given him a literal answer.

He was essentially shy. He said that you never lose people you love when they die, because you incorporate parts of their personalities into your own as a means of keeping them alive. It was in his mother's nature to be interested socially in the lives of other people, and when he found himself taking pleasure in talking to strangers at parties, he was aware that the impulse could be traced to her.

He had been mindful since childhood of his differences from other people — his sensitivity, his social awkwardness, his preference for reading over being outdoors, his slight frame, his partiality for solitude, his love of classical music and especially opera, the way that having lost his mother left him with a mark that seemed visible to other people. The couple in *The Chateau*, Harold and Barbara Rhodes, resemble the Maxwells. Of Harold Rhodes, Maxwell wrote, "He was thin, flat-chested, narrow-faced, pale from lack of sleep, and tense in his movements. A whole generation of loud, confident Middle-Western voices saying: Harold, sit up straight . . . Harold, hold your shoulders back . . . Harold, you need a haircut, you look like a violinist had had no effect whatever. Confidence had slipped through his fingers. He had failed to be like other people."

It is hard to be an original person, an individual. No one cares for it, really. Very few people will congratulate you on the accomplishment. At close hand a truly original person is almost always disturbing. Indulgent and self-consciously outrageous behavior, show business boy and girl behavior — attitudes and mannerisms summoned in the attempt to bring notice to a negligible personality — is not the same as being original, because it is necessarily in response to something. A reaction to someone else's point of view. Someone's standards have to be outraged, and once you figure out what they consist of, it's simple to come up with a means of insulting them. It's a tactic for drawing notice, of not being overlooked, and the people who engage in it generally have little of what is required to hold one's attention once they have it. Anyone who is truly original is likely to be taunted, made fun of, his point of view being so divergent from the ordinary, the accepted. An easy mark for torment. He is likely to be to one side or the other of your awareness, not directly in front of anyone's gaze, unless he wasn't able to move out of the way quickly enough. His appearance probably does not matter much to him. His mind is too preoccupied to care about his clothes or whether his haircut is fashionable. He is not likely to care for having people know too much about him, preferring to operate as a subversive. His intentions surely undermine those of the common grain. They don't embrace the rule, the popular or the conventional, and he only feels the restraints such considerations impose.

Maxwell never made a gesture to bring himself or his writing to anyone's notice, and he didn't allow any to be made on his behalf. Such behavior would have pained him.

From his daughters, I know that Maxwell had a temper, but I never saw it. Somewhere he says that it was of the annihilating kind, and that in his heart he knew he was capable of murder. When he was a boy, he grabbed a golf iron and ran after his older brother who had teased him one time too many, and was intercepted before he could lay him out. If he said no, you knew the decision was final, and that it was worthless to try to dissuade him. He did not waste anyone's time and did not like having his wasted, although he was tolerant and so considerate of another person's feelings that he often ended up doing something he didn't want to in order to avoid causing someone discomfort or unhappiness.

Maxwell wrote his second novel, *They Came Like Swallows*, in several places: Mrs. Green's farm in Wisconsin, the MacDowell Colony, and in an upstairs bedroom of the Buseys' house in Urbana, where he graded papers in exchange for room and board. He finished the book when he was twenty-eight and then went back to New York, in 1936, to look for a job.

"My father had given me a hundred dollars, and I had another hundred I didn't tell him about," he said. "I went to a friend of his, the president of an insurance company, to get the check cashed. He had always before been friendly and fatherly to me, and this time he surprised me by being harsh and telling me I had no business trying to get a job in New York, that I wouldn't make it here, and had better get back to my long-haired friends in Wisconsin. About whom he actually knew nothing. From someone at MacDowell I had been given letters of introduction to *The New Republic* and to *Time*, and my editor at Harper had called Katharine White at *The New Yorker* and asked if she would see me. I went first to *The New Republic*, and it took them only a few minutes to realize that I didn't have a political thought in my head. And it took three weeks to receive an appointment with the personnel office at *Time*. Meanwhile, my father's friend had made me so furious that I talked myself into a job reading novels for Paramount Pictures. The first book they gave me was called *Lady Cynthia Candon's Husband*. It was seven hundred pages, and they wanted my account to be five pages long — single- or double-spaced I don't remember — with five carbons. It took me two days to read the book and another day to summarize the action, and then I took it to be typed, since there was very little time left, which cost five dollars. Because it was a long book they gave me a special price of seven-fifty, leaving two-fifty in the clear for three days' work.

Then they gave me a second book, which I remember nothing about, and then I went for an interview with Katharine White.

"Wolcott Gibbs, an editor involved with both writers and artists, had grown weary of part of his job, and they were looking for somebody to take his place in the art meeting and convey to the artists, who came in the next day, that their covers and drawings and spots had been bought — which meant usually that there were suggestions for the picture or the caption and sometimes meant that the drawings had to be done over because of some detail that could not be corrected otherwise. Or that they were rejected. And this, nobody needed to tell me, had to be done in such a way that they were not unduly discouraged.

"I hadn't been reading *The New Yorker* at all. The fact that I had published a novel and had another ready to be published and had had a story in *The Atlantic* must have worked in my favor. I was twenty-eight and straight out of the Middle West. I don't really remember how I conducted myself; I was interested, leaned forward in my chair, what you do in interviews. Instinct made me keep silent about a significant part of my past; teaching school, I somehow knew, would not be a mark in my favor. At the end of the interview, Mrs. White asked how much I would want in the way of a salary. I had been told by a knowledgeable friend that I must ask for thirty-five dollars, that they wouldn't respect me unless I did.

So I took a deep breath and said thirty-five dollars, and she smiled and said, 'I expect you could live on less.' I could have lived nicely on fifteen. I couldn't make out whether the interview had been favorable or not. The thought of reading manuscripts for the movies didn't make me cheerful. I was living on the top floor of a brownstone rooming house on Lexington and Thirty-sixth Street, or thereabouts. I remember the mattress was lumpy, and there were bedbugs. I went down to the Village and wandered around and decided to eat dinner at a Chinese restaurant on Eighth Street, and though there were empty tables, they made me sit with another person. In a bottomless depression I said to myself, there is no place for me anywhere in the world. And after dinner came home and under my door was a telegram from Mrs. White that read, 'Come to work on Monday at the price agreed upon.'"

The New Yorker was eleven years old and had got itself out of financial difficulties and was one of the few places in New York that were untouched by the Depression. "There was a shortage of office space at the time," Maxwell said, "and my desk, in a corner of the rather large outer office where Mrs. White's secretary cracked the whip on a couple of unfortunate stenographers, was right next to Mrs. White's door, which remained open until she had a visitor, in which case she would rise from her desk and, while talking, release the catch. There were quite a number of visitors, and between the arrival of the visitor and the closing of the door my education into the workings of the magazine advanced at an interesting pace."

On Mondays there was nothing for Maxwell to do. He sat at his desk and looked at a self-portrait by James Thurber drawn in pencil on the wall in front of him. Thurber's drawings were all over the premises. By a water cooler in a corner of a hallway was a drawing of a man walking along in a carefree way and around the corner was a woman waiting for him with a baseball bat held above her head.

"On Tuesdays," Maxwell told me, "the artists — as they were called; actually they were cartoonists — brought their work in, and Tuesday afternoon the art meeting took place, in a room large enough to hold a big table and four chairs. The drawings were propped up so that they could be seen, and everybody had knitting needles, of plastic, to point to details of the drawings. I had one, but didn't use it. Harold Ross was in charge. By common agreement 'roughs,' that is, drawings that indicated what the picture would be like but were only sketches, were rejected or approved — if approved, the artist would make a finished drawing and submit it the following week. Though it was still the best period of *New Yorker* cartoonists, more often than not the ideas were forced. Since they were one-line jokes, Ross was concerned that the speaker be immediately identifiable. Sometimes the captions were changed. Or if there was a good drawing with a bad caption, it was sent to E. B.

White, who was responsible for some of the most fa-mous lines. Most of the ideas were so forced that I found the meeting deadly. Also, I suffered from insomnia and was afraid if I didn't sleep the night before the art meet-ing I wouldn't know whether something was funny or not. I would look into the mirror at home while I shaved and say, I hope I will recognize what's funny. There're two kinds of humor, the spontaneous, which I am able to get, and the manufactured kind, Perelman, which does nothing for me."

On Wednesdays Maxwell sat beside Rea Irvin, the art editor, while he looked at the spot drawings. "If I liked a drawing," Maxwell said, "he good-naturedly put it in the yes pile." On Thursdays the artists retrieved their draw-ings, and Maxwell spent the day with one after another of them. "What was odd was that the artists all put themselves in their pictures, so that when they arrived for the first time I was perfectly familiar with them."

Since Maxwell's job took only a day and a half, mercy suggested that a way be found to keep him busy. Mrs. White told him to read the magazine's scrapbooks, and not long after that he was given some manuscripts to read and express his opinions about. "Then I was told I could write some letters of rejection, which I was to leave with Mrs. White's secretary. The next day she called me into her office and closed the door and said, indicat-ing the letters of rejection, 'Mr. Maxwell, did you ever teach school?' Without realizing I was doing it, I had betrayed my secret. I had to confess that for two years I taught freshman composition at the University of Illinois while working toward a Ph.D. that I never got. Very kindly she explained there was a difference between writers, good or bad, and students, and I must not seem, in my letters, to be telling writers how to write."

Mrs. White also encouraged him to submit stories to the magazine. Being on the inside and seeing the opinion sheets accompanying the manuscripts sent to Ross, Maxwell felt he fairly well understood the sort of material the magazine was looking for and was able to give them what they wanted — "Valentines that arrived on the wrong day, that sort of thing," he said. When he was happy for the check but felt that the story seemed slight or involved people who might recognize themselves when he didn't want them to, he published the story as Jonathan Harrington or as Gifford Brown.

For a while Maxwell worked under Gibbs, preparing authors' proofs, getting rid of what copy editors had added when they were being too pedantic, and removing some of the less sensible queries. "Ross was perceptive about fiction," he said, "and his few comments on a given manuscript were usually to the point. But when he read the story again in galleys, it was quite a different matter. Having the whole magazine to read, he read too fast, misread, or misremembered details and then tried to make things consistent with what the author hadn't, in fact, written. His proofs usually had fifty or sixty queries, of which four were inspired, and the rest were a waste of time. The proofreader's pedantries would have outraged the authors, if they had been permitted to see them, so I was given the job of screening the proofs to save Mrs. White and Gibbs from having to deal with the authors, and by observing how they dealt with the queries, I began to learn what editing was.

"The pieces given to me to edit were usually slight entertaining ones for the back of the book — the kind of thing people liked to read before falling asleep. The writers were seldom accomplished. The most prolific was Joseph Wechsberg, who was European and had been a ship's violinist and had a seemingly endless background to draw on, but his understanding of English syntax was imperfect, and turning his sentences into acceptable prose was backbreaking work."

Gibbs's mind worked quickly, and Maxwell hardly ever finished a question before Gibbs had already answered it. "He was always patient with me," Maxwell said, "and flared up only once, over a detail about a cocktail. I said I didn't know anything about such drinks, and he took it, for a second, as a criticism of him until he realized it was only the simple truth.

"Anyway, when I began dealing with galley proofs, they gave me an office at last. Somewhere along in the first three months I felt I was going to be fine, and sent back my father's hundred dollars. When he got it, my stepmother said, he wept. He was a businessman. The concept of literature was outside his experience and beyond his understanding, so he had no idea really what

I was up to. It had been the great fear of his life that I would be financially irresponsible and sponge off other people."

After Maxwell had been at *The New Yorker* for a year or so, he went to dinner at the Plaza Hotel with a cousin from the Midwest who was two years older than he was. The cousin was married and had a twelve-year-old daughter and was a stockbroker — that is, his life was very different from Maxwell's. They knew each other only slightly. The cousin asked questions that Maxwell answered politely but sententiously, leaving the cousin to choose between asking another question or having the two of them eat in silence. Maxwell was under the impression that the cousin had invited him to dinner because he felt that he ought to, "whereas in fact," Maxwell writes in *Ancestors,* his family history, "it was because something — that I was a misfit introverted child, that he was fond of my mother and father, that I represented the younger brother he wished he had had — made him interested in me. All I know for sure, and I wish I had known it on that occasion, is that he was immensely pleased and proud of me because I had published a couple of novels."

Ancestors was written twenty-five years later, and in it Maxwell describes the dinner with his cousin and allows himself to say what he might have if he hadn't held himself back.

"I was living in a rooming house on Lexington

Avenue and I had dinner with somebody from the office who said there was a vacant apartment in the building where he lived, so I went home with him, and the door was unlocked but there weren't any light bulbs, and I took it because I liked the way it felt in the dark. The rent is thirty-five dollars a month. You go past an iron gate into a courtyard with gas streetlamps. It was built during the Civil War, I think. Anyway, it's very old. And my apartment is on the third floor, looking out on a different courtyard, with trees in it. Ailanthus trees. I like having something green to look at. Technically it's a room and a half. The half is a bedroom just big enough for a single bed, and I never sleep there because it's too like lying in a coffin. I sleep on a studio couch in the living room. The fireplace works. And once when I had done something I was terribly ashamed of, I went and put my forehead on the mantelpiece. It was just the right height.

"The kitchen is tiny, but it has a skylight that opens. And by putting one foot on the edge of the sink and the other on top of the icebox I can pull myself up onto the roof, and I sit there sometimes looking at the moon and the stars. In the morning, when I'm shaving, I hear the prostitutes being brought to the women's prison. Shouting and screaming. Though I'm on a courtyard, it's never really quiet in New York the way it is in the country. Just as I'm drifting off at night I hear a taxi horn. Or I hear the Sixth Avenue El, and try to fall asleep before the next one comes. The building directly across from my windows is some kind of a factory, and in the daytime when the workmen come out and stand on the fire escape talking, and when the doors are open, I can hear the clicking of the machinery. At night there is a cat that sits on the fire escape and makes hideous sounds like a baby having its throat cut, until I get up and throw beer bottles at it. If I don't get any sleep I'm no good at my job. It's an interesting job and I like it and I'm lucky to have it, but I have to deal with so many people all day long that when night comes I don't want to see any-body. When the telephone rings, which isn't very often, I don't answer it. I let it ring and ring and finally it stops, and the silence then is so beautiful. I read, or I walk the streets until I'm dead tired and come home hoping to fall asleep. At the far end of the courtyard there's an intern from St. Vincent's Hospital who never pulls his shades. I see his light go on about eleven. He has a girl — she is so nice — she brought him a balloon when he was sick. But there is another girl she doesn't know about who sleeps with him too. Next to the factory, on the sec-ond floor, there is a young married couple. In the morn-ing when I'm drinking my coffee by the window, the sunlight reaches far enough into their apartment for me to see the shapes of their bodies under the bedclothes. Sometimes she comes to the window in her nightgown or her slip and stands brushing her hair. You can tell they're in love because their movements are so heavy. As if they were drugged. And once I saw him sitting in his undershorts putting on his socks. Everything they do is like a painting.

"I tried to get a job in New York once before, in 1933, before my first book was published, and couldn't. It was like trying to climb a glass mountain. The book had two favorable reviews, but it didn't cause any commercial excitement whatever, so I went home and started another novel, and when that petered out, I started another, and made my savings stretch as far as possible, and took help from my friends. Not money. Room and board, in exchange for doing things for them that they were perfectly able to do for themselves. This was so I wouldn't feel obligated. When I finished the second book I came back here and this time I managed to stay. But my job takes up so much of my energy that I write less and less. I can do stories, but that's all. And not many of them.

"I've fallen in love three times in my life, and each time it was with someone who wasn't in love with me, and now I can't do it any more. I have friends. There's a place uptown where I can go when I feel like being with people, and the door is never locked; you just walk in and go through the apartment till you find somebody, and they set an extra place at the dinner table for me without asking, and so I don't feel nobody cares if I live or die. But I can't sleep at night because when I put out my hands there isn't anybody in the bed beside me, and it's as if I'd exchanged one glass mountain for another, and I don't know what to do . . ."

*

Gibbs withdrew more and more from his editing job into profile writing and also from the art meeting and insofar as Maxwell was able to he took his place. "With a raise," Maxwell said. "Every time I was promoted I would go to him and ask how much I should ask for, and he always told me the right answer. When I went to Bermuda for my vacation and came back wearing loafers and a sport jacket I bought and with dark glasses on, he passed me in the hall and said, not unkindly, 'The shoes or the jacket but not both.' The people who made the magazine were half a generation older than I was, and they came of age in the twenties. And I came of age in the thirties, it was a much more serious period, so though I was not uncomfortable with them, I didn't belong to them. I was extremely naïve, and they all seemed so sophisticated. They all talked about Noël Coward openings every night at seven-thirty. It was not that they were more sophisticated; I just didn't share their interests.

"Somewhere along about my second year I had a telephone call from my editor at Harper saying that *They Came Like Swallows* had been chosen as a dual selection of the Book-of-the-Month Club, and the initial payment was eight thousand dollars. It was so much money, in 1937, I had to lean against the wall for support. I went and told Gibbs. And then I invited the Whites to dinner and the theater. I asked Gibbs where to take them, and he told me. It was small and the most elegant restaurant by far that I had ever been in. I took what was the most imaginable cash to pay for it — thirty-five dollars and that's exactly what it came to."

Around that time Maxwell was taken out of the fiction department and made A-issue editor, which meant that he worked with Ross on assembling each week's issue. "I loved working with him," Maxwell said. "He was very funny and not the bore that he is sometimes made out to be. I had been told that in a fit of temper he once threw a telephone at Mrs. White, but he never even raised his voice at me. Once I told him something that I thought was correct only to find, when I left his office, that I should have given him the exact contrary advice. I remember leaning against the door and thinking I can't go in and tell him my answer was wrong. Then my upbringing asserted itself and I went in and told him I had given him the wrong information, and he didn't turn a hair. He wasn't interested in my mistake, only in the right answer."

Gibbs was made the magazine's theater critic, which meant that his job working with Mrs. White in the fiction department was open, and Maxwell took it, which allowed him to return to editing manuscripts. "Then Andy White began to be restless and went to live in Maine," Maxwell said, "which meant that Katharine had to leave the job she had created and was very happy in. *The New Yorker* hired a friend of Andy's, Gus Lobrano, who was working on *Town and Country*, and I took him into my office to break him in, and we became friends. I suppose this was around 1942. I assumed I would replace Mrs. White as fiction editor, which was pure foolishness on my part, because the job was just as much a matter of dealing with humorists, perhaps more so, than fiction writers. When my uncle died, in Illinois, and I went to the funeral, I came back to find that Lobrano had been moved into Mrs. White's office, which meant he was slated to become her successor. I thought, The hell with them, I will become a writer if that's the way things are. So I asked for an appointment with Ross to tell him I was resigning, and he invited me, for the first time, to lunch at the Algonquin. We sat down to a table and I told him I wanted to leave, and he said, 'I was going to offer you the job of second-in-command of the magazine.' Which rocked me a little, but he didn't urge me to reconsider, and if I had it would have meant that very soon I wouldn't have been working for the magazine at all, because the second-in-command always got blamed for whatever went wrong and sooner or later was fired."

When Maxwell quit *The New Yorker*, he went to New Mexico with a friend, Morris Birge, who had taken a house for the summer in Sante Fe. Birge was engaged to a woman there and was very social, but Maxwell asked not to be introduced to anyone, and over the course of the summer he recovered himself.

As to how he passed the time, one day he sat down at the typewriter and wrote:

"Almost no sleep last night, though I didn't mind. I

lay on one side and then the other and eventually, as I thought I might, dreamt of home. The Rio Grande flows through the front yard but it is smaller than the creek where we used to go fishing, when I was a child. The geography books didn't say it would be like that, hemmed in by mesas, and likely before the summer comes to be even smaller . . .

"Yesterday morning the Spanish-American gardener cleaned out the winter's dust and rotting leaves from the fishpond, and while Morris and I sat on our haunches, watching him catch the big gold fish and the five little ones that had no color, in a white granite pan, I thought what a good beginning page for a book. I still think in beginnings, like a man forever putting on his hat. To think of the end instead of the beginning has been for a long time — I don't know how long, twenty years perhaps — to think of death. And because I don't want to think of it, or write of it, not through fear but now, I think, merely from choice, my direction is toward the beginnings of things. But it is an obvious kind of near-sightedness, and there must obviously be exercises to correct it. When I raised my eyes a minute ago I saw a windmill a hundred yards away, and it was revolving steadily in the sunlight, without any beginning and probably, for years to come, without any end. The air is never quite still here, and the windmill may slow up — is now — but I don't think it will stop. But how to do that? How to write a book that will go round and round, faster or slower, without a beginning or an end, but only night and day and night and day. The windmill is absolutely still. Now it is going quite fast again, proving that an end which is followed immediately by a beginning is neither end nor beginning but a continuity of a different kind, a rhythm that is more accurate, as an analogy, to living, than continuous revolving, which can only have a single meaning.

"Realized yesterday, watching through binoculars a gardener mowing grass that the reality we accept through the senses is almost never perceived by one sense alone. A man mowing grass should be accompanied by the sound of a lawnmower, to be believed. Because the air is thin and clear, and because of the binoculars one can separate the sense of sight and the sense of hearing from their usual union. And then merely by closing one's eyes the man mowing the lawn becomes an idea only, and one has to look to the mind for confirmation of his actuality, not to the senses. Which may account for the inward look on the faces of the blind, and the strained expression of the deaf. With the failure of sight and hearing to confirm one another, both the blind and the deaf must depend upon general knowledge, must go continually to the mind for evidence, rather than for the meaning of the evidence they have received through sensory perception. And the boundary between the natural and the supernatural (which is mostly suspected by the fact that the senses don't jibe) must be far less, though to a different degree, the blind falling back upon the sense of touch, the deaf making the eyes do the work of both seeing and hearing. To both a great many things cannot exist.

"And in one way or another, for large sections of all time, we are either blind or deaf, sometimes both. A man passed the house this morning, and I saw him out of the bathroom window; saw him returning with a little girl in blue overalls. And even so I failed to perceive that his wife had died this morning. A blind man might have heard it in his step, a deaf person in the way he turned his face to the sun. But all I saw was a man getting older and heavier before it was time for him to get old and heavy."

When Maxwell got back to New York, Lobrano called and said it was lonely at the office without him and could he send some manuscripts to him for his opinion. After about a month of this arrangement, Maxwell decided it would be easier to go to the office to read them, so he began working there three days a week.

If we live long enough, our lives make some sort of sensible pattern. For much of his life, Maxwell had friendships with older women, such as Zona Gale, Garreta Busey, and Sylvia Townsend Warner, which gave him a steadying guidance. The poet Louise Bogan was *The New Yorker*'s poetry critic and dealt with Mrs. White. When she expressed admiration for one of Maxwell's stories, Mrs. White introduced them. Bogan was fifteen years older than Maxwell and had stopped writing poetry after a severe mental breakdown. Maxwell admired her immensely. He went to see her in her apartment, and she played songs of Mahler and Hugo Wolf, music he didn't know, and they talked about Yeats and Rilke. Maxwell showed her the manuscript of a story about some boys in a high school swimming pool, and she said that he should continue with it — that it was a novel. It became *The Folded Leaf,* and the story became the novel's first chapter. He did four versions, which he sent, chapter by chapter, to Bogan, and she made very few criticisms but simply wrote back, "Keep on."

The notes he made in New Mexico found a place in the novel's pattern.

Maxwell's years on the Wisconsin farm left him with a love of country living. A friend visiting his apartment noticed the geraniums on the windowsill and suggested that Maxwell find himself a house. He had a chance to rent an 1840 saltbox house on the quiet road in northern Westchester where my father lived, and he gave up his apartment, on Patchin Place, and commuted to the office. The house had been rented by a Southern family whose habits of housekeeping were so slovenly that the insurance on the house had been canceled and they were evicted. To move out, they placed open suitcases on the lawn and threw shoes and clothes out the second-floor window into them. Maxwell painted the trim and began planting flowerbeds, and the house was sold out from under him. Then he bought the house down the road from the house my parents lived in.

When he was nearly through *The Folded Leaf*, he was drafted. "I didn't want to go to war," he said. "I was a pacifist, and I didn't want to get shot. The Army didn't recognize pacifism unless it was attached to some church. So I went to a psychiatrist and got a letter. What the letter said was that I had an anxiety neurosis. I waited around and nobody read it. I got on the boat to Governors Island and went to the induction center. I went through every step except the psychiatrist. Finally, when I was all but inducted, someone was willing to read my letter. He was a European and he said, "'Sweet are the uses of adversity.' Who said that?' and I said, 'Shakespeare, but I don't know where,' and he said, 'As You Like It,' and stamped my papers, and that was that."

One day in early 1945 Lobrano came into Maxwell's office and told him that Ross had heard that Maxwell was halfway through a novel he had been working on for several years and was having difficulty finishing, with all that was expected of him at the office, so Ross was sending him home for six months on full pay. Ross was in the habit of doing kind things and then disclaiming them. Maxwell eventually asked why he had done him such a favor, and Ross said that he played poker with another writer who was always talking about never having the time to finish anything, and he had merely been thinking of that.

Once the book had been handed in to the publisher, Maxwell returned to the office. Ross asked whether he would read unsolicited manuscripts, the slush pile, and though it was a wearing job, Maxwell felt he could hardly say no. He usually found one story a month that the magazine could print.

A year or so before Maxwell died, I said to him, "You seem so untroubled," and he said, "I am now." In his early thirties, unhappy at having such a solitary life, he went, on the advice of a friend, to see the psychoanalyst Theodor Reik, who had studied with Freud. "I had too great a sense of my own difference from other people," he said. "After about a year of talking to Reik five days a week, and hearing his voice occasionally respond from behind my shoulder, the whole first part of my life fell away, and I had a sense of everyone's similarities. I had a feeling of starting again. Instead of being recessive and introverted, I suddenly had a clue to what other people are like. Given the situation, you can pretty much figure out what they're going through, and it's usually something that involves sympathy and understanding. You can't possibly have a sense of understanding somebody without feeling sympathetic.

"After I stopped talking to him and felt the need for it, I sat down for two days at the typewriter, and what came out was very strange. I decided that I was so angry at my parents for having another child — why aren't they satisfied with me — that I thought they should die and then be brought back. I damn near accomplished it with my father, who also got the flu, but I lost my mother. So I was a murderer. And what do you do with murderers? You put them in a cell. I was in a cell — no wife, no family. I was in a prison cell, and there was Reik saying, You're in a prison cell, but the door's not locked."

Lying awake one night in the house in Westchester, Maxwell remembered a young woman who had come to his office a year and a half earlier, looking for a position in the poetry department. "She wore her hair piled on top of her head," he said, "and she had a hat with a fur piece — it was winter, I suppose — and I thought I had never seen anyone so beautiful, but I did nothing about it. It was as if I was in a deep sleep."

The next day he looked for her name — Emily Noyes — in the phone book, and it wasn't there, but she had left her number with the magazine's personnel office, and on the disingenuous pretext of wanting to talk to her about her poetry, he asked her for a drink at the Algonquin. She was from a prosperous family in Portland, Oregon; she was teaching two-year-olds at a nursery school on the Upper East Side; and she lived in a room on the top floor of the building. Maxwell was thirty-six, and she was twenty-three, tall and thin, with black hair and a wide face and dark eyes so lively that people often took her and Maxwell for sister and brother. It was the fall, and he invited her to a party at the house of a friend, and they talked all evening, and when he took her home he asked her to marry him. He hadn't planned on saying it; the words simply came out of his mouth. She said that she didn't want to get married and that she wouldn't be able to see him again until after the first of the year, but he could telephone her at the nursery school between four-fifteen and four-thirty. After that she would be dealing with parents.

At four-fifteen Maxwell closed the door of his office and began dialing. More often than not the school line was busy, but sometimes he got through to her. In January he closed his house and rented a one-room apartment that had been converted from a doctor's office, and began courting her. They were married in May of 1945, in the chapel of the Presbyterian Church at Fifth Avenue and Twelfth Street.

When Maxwell brought her home to Illinois so that his father and stepmother could meet her, his father took him aside after a few days and said, "There has been no one like her in our family for generations."

Someone with her radiance is what he meant. Also, her graceful and unassuming way of conducting herself. Also, her fine carriage, which I think of as having been molded in childhood by holding herself upright on horseback. As a child she rode a horse to school.

She was nearly always the most beautiful woman of any age in a room of other women, although I am not aware that she ever made any effort to be. Her face was suffused with an illumination that seemed to concentrate itself in her eyes. I am reminded of the labels at the Frick Museum that mention the illusion that Rembrandt's portraits appear to be lit from within.

With his wife in mind, Maxwell wrote of Barbara Rhodes in *The Chateau:* "Because she came of a family that seemed to produce handsomeness no matter what hereditary strains it was crossed with, the turn of the forehead, the coloring, the carving of the eyelids, the fine bones, the beautiful carriage could all be accounted for by people with long memories. But it was the eyes that you noticed. They were dark brown, and widely spaced, and very large, and full of light, the way children's eyes are, the eyebrows naturally arched, the upper eyelids wide but not heavy, not weighted, the whites a blue white. If all her other features had been bad, she still would have seemed beautiful because of them. They were the eyes of someone of another Age, their expression now gentle and direct, now remote, so far from calculating, and yet intelligent, perceptive, pessimistic, without guile, and without coquetry."

And: "As a rule, the men who turned to stare at Barbara Rhodes in public places were generally of a romantic disposition or else old enough to be her father. Even more than her appearance, her voice attracted and disturbed them, reminding them of what they themselves had been like at her age, or throwing them headlong into an imaginary conversation with her, or making them wonder whether in giving the whole of their affection to one woman they had settled for less than they might have got if they had had the courage and the patience to go on looking. But this was not true here. In the eyes that were turned toward her, there was no recognition of who she was but only of the one simple use that she could be put to."

I never heard from my father that Maxwell had stood over another man's chair at a dinner party and said, "Will you leave now?" but there must have been occasions when other men stared too fixedly at her or kept her on the dance floor longer than was polite.

I can imagine two empty chairs at a table set for dinner and someone's asking, "Who else are we waiting for?" and the hostess replying, "The Maxwells. He's a writer, and an editor at *The New Yorker,* and their daughters are at school with Jessica (or, We were introduced to them this summer on the Vineyard; or, Emmy goes to the Art Students League with Rachel), and I've wanted you to meet them." And the Maxwells arriving, with apologies for being late (the difficulty of getting a taxi in the East Eighties at the hour when everyone is heading to the theater), and the men, having been impatient and distracted, sitting suddenly straighter in their chairs.

She was long-limbed and lean and girlish. Seated on a couch, she had a way of pulling her knees up beneath her and gathering her skirt around them that was like the gesture of an adolescent.

I have photographs of her, taken by my father, at parties on the road where the Maxwells and my parents lived, when she was perhaps twenty-four, just married, and smoking a cigarette and leaning back on the couch, wearing a sweater and a skirt to just below her knees — New Year's, I think it was, or someone's birthday. She is wearing a particular high-heeled black shoe that has a strap around her ankle, and her hair is black and her eyes are shining, and I think, There would be a problem taking her out in public. Men would want to steal her away, might even resolve to. Everyone else in the photographs is older, and much as she liked them, I also imagine she was a little restless in their company. She had a great enthusiasm for fun and was of an age to embrace it. She once told my wife that she spent a lot of her first year married alone in the house in the country while Maxwell was at his office in the city, and that she taught herself to cook by reading cookbooks to pass the time. It was not likely the life she had come East for. The photographs of her in scrapbooks from her childhood show her as a girl surrounded by boys with strong jaws and physiques that I associate with the phrase physical culture. The sort of boys who came home in the 1940s wearing soldiers' outfits.

For a while before she met Maxwell, she was involved with the writer James Agee. Smoking cigarettes and drinking whiskey and talking late into the night is how I imagine them, his eyes falling on her and him finding it difficult to believe his luck.

Because she ran the household, and because she loved reading, especially poetry — Rilke and Neruda and Roethke above all — going to museums and movies, and conversation, the dance classes she took at her ladies club, and the company of her family and friends, it was difficult for her to spend as many hours in her studio as she wanted to. She began drawing as a young woman, and when her daughters were grown she turned seriously to painting. She matured quickly, and in the last years had a breakthrough. She favored a dark and luxurious palette. Her attention was meticulous. A still life depicting a hand of solitaire, interrupted; the phone rang, or the person playing heard his name called. Or lost interest. Something took him away, anyhow, and the painting records the way things looked in the interval before he returned, when they were suspended, like a chord in music waiting to be resolved.

The one I am most drawn to is an oil crayon drawing of an old fish that was too crafty to be caught, remembered, I think, from her childhood, a legendary trout. Under the river, with the trees on the banks and the water flowing around him, and him flipping his tail exuberantly. It was, I think, a study for a painting that was never made.

She once said that she planned to spend her old age having two drinks at lunch at the Cosmopolitan Club and falling asleep afterward in one of the club's chairs, with her mouth open. She had a spiritual side, and Maxwell didn't believe in God. She wanted to work for the

Partisan Review, and she liked William Burroughs — *The Naked Lunch,* anyway. She loved the faux cowboy song "Don't Fence Me In." She used to play it on the jukeboxes in Third Avenue saloons where Maxwell followed her when they were courting. Dropping coins into the slots, she must have wondered why this man with his own beautiful eyes pursued her so ardently, as if his life depended on it. I don't think he ever felt truly happy until he married her.

They loved each other in a way that most of us cannot appreciate at first hand — that is, a marriage of fifty-five years as intimate as theirs was is not something most people will experience. They were like two trees whose roots have grown together.

Maxwell once dreamed that he flew to Paris in a box, and when he saw how beautiful Paris was he flew back to get her.

Years ago, to my father, Maxwell wrote: "Emmy's father had a slight stroke, complicated or rather followed by pneumonia and pleurisy, which is surely enough, with emphysema and a not too good heart, to do any ordinary man of almost 92 in, but he isn't ordinary, and has recovered from worse. Anyway, she went off to Oregon this morning . . . She left at 9:15 and it is now 3:25 P.M. and you can hear a pin drop. Only there is nobody to drop it. Ordinarily I am home alone all day and never feel that the apartment is queer or empty because I know Emmy will be home from the Art Students League at six o'clock. But because she is somewhere in the air over I suppose Montana this place is uninhabitable."

On his desk in the country Maxwell kept a small painted box, a present from her on his ninetieth birthday. On the cover of the box she painted a lion lounging in the branches of a tree. On the bottom of the box she wrote, "Each day I am as glad to see you as I am to see the sun rise in the morning and the moon cross the sky at night."

Saintly is what I sometimes thought they were, but they weren't, of course. Maxwell occasionally affected a saintly manner to deflect attention he wasn't interested in. What was so admirable to me about the manner in which they conducted their lives — the courtesy to others, the care for other people's difficulties, and their belief that we should do what we can to help each other — was that the way they acted, the gestures they made, were choices and decisions arrived at in an atmosphere of distractions and social considerations and awareness of consequences and opportunities passed on and perhaps lost. When a choice was to be made, it seemed to me, so far as I knew, that the Maxwells always made one that demonstrated character and judgment and the restraint of self-interest, and that was likely to have been influenced by a concern for someone else's feelings. Out of a desire to protect them, I often urged them to be more cold-blooded, but they wouldn't be.

They were everything that ordinary life is not. Not envious. Not resentful, not trivial, not obstructive of other people's happiness. Not shrill in their enthusiasms. Not strident, mean, or coarse in their sentiments. Not indifferent to suffering. Their lives had no fewer difficulties than anyone else's, and yet they gave the appearance that everything came effortlessly to them. No gesture they made was performed for effect. They had no personas. They were not calculating. Neither of them had an impulse toward self-inflation. They had no social ambitions beyond the company of people they admired and cared for. They were handsome but not vain. They loved expressions of enthusiasm. Although they were prosperous, they weren't materialistic, and they were always mindful of how money might ease a difficulty in someone's life or bring them some happiness. Checks now and then left the household in amounts that substantially changed the circumstances of the people who cashed them. Once, in the manner of Elvis Presley, Maxwell gave one of my brothers a car.

In 1947, Maxwell sent to Cyril Connolly, the British critic and editor of the magazine *Horizon,* a story he had written about a family of Southerners who paid a visit during the summer of 1912 to their Northern relatives. Connolly wrote to him: "Dear Maxwell: After considerable thought I returned your ms. to your agent here because I decided the story you sent me was really a very exciting beginning to a novel, especially as the period was 1912, and you simply couldn't leave things where they were. One wants another thirty chapters, and I hope you will do it that way.

"It was the Emperor Augustus whose last words were something like 'Do you think I have played out the comedy correctly?' I can't quote the Latin, which you will find in Suetonius' life of Augustus.

"Please understand that I mean exactly what I say about the story, and I am not being polite. It is too good a situation to leave in the air. Continue!

My regards to your beautiful wife . . ."

A few months later, Maxwell wrote to his father-in-law: "I took an important step yesterday that I want to tell you about. For the last six months I have been straining against the burden of a double life, of working at a somewhat demanding job and trying to write a novel. It is never easy to give half your heart to one thing and half to another, and after a good deal of thought I have told *The New Yorker* that I want to leave, the first of May . . .

"We have put aside a sum of money for emergencies, and we ought to be able to live essentially as we do now, on the money I make from writing. If not, I can always go back to *The New Yorker,* where I am useful both as an editor and as a writer. During the last two years I have made as much from writing as I have from my job . . ."

He stayed away less than a year. "I had thought I would write more and better if I did nothing but write," he told me, "and I was selling enough stories to live on, and I had some savings, and I thought we could skid by, and the first thing that happened was we needed a new refrigerator, and the second thing that happened is that the stories I wrote weren't being taken. It helped to know what the magazine wanted, but not infallibly. Even though I saw what they wanted, I didn't necessarily want to give it to them. I had more serious things on my mind. But then I looked at my fortieth birthday approaching and I thought I ought to insinuate myself back onto the staff."

The academic who asked Maxwell about the most exciting moments of his career also asked what moment was the most disappointing. Maxwell answered, "Pass." I never heard him express envy for the sales or prizes of another writer. *The Chateau* was nominated for the National Book Award, which was won by Walker Percy, for *The Moviegoer*. Maxwell attended the reception after the ceremony, and Percy endeared himself to him by saying, when they met, "My wife has been reading me passages from your novel all afternoon in our hotel room."

Because Maxwell lived so long, he continued into what might partly have been his posterity, so he got to see the wide and widening appreciation of his work, but if his books had been less admired, he might have been forced to face their oblivion. Maxwell's success was more literary than commercial, and the two don't often intersect. In *The Enemies of Promise*, Cyril Connolly wrote that a classic is a book that remains in print for ten years. *They Came Like Swallows* has been more than sixty years in print. After Maxwell died, I had a letter from the novelist Shirley Hazzard in which she mentioned the disparity between his literary standing and his commercial accomplishments. "Only a saint could have borne with complete equanimity the inadequate recognition he had for years to endure," she wrote. "He knew it was incommensurate, unjust. He stayed with the truth that was in him, developing it throughout his life."

It would only have been natural for him to have felt discouraged by *The New Yorker*'s not buying the stories he hoped that they would. The story Connolly admired became *Time Will Darken It*. A few years later, in 1955, Maxwell went through what I think was the only period of resignation he experienced; at least he never told me about another. "It was when Kate" — his older daughter — "was a baby," he said. "I thought, I might just as well stop writing and be a full-time editor. I guess I hadn't any novel on hand that interested me, and I did fewer and fewer stories. It looked as if I was running dry, but I wasn't. I needed a little public encouragement.

"I had set my heart a few years before on the Pulitzer Prize for *Time Will Darken It*, and the National Book Award, if there was such a thing then, or its equivalent. I wanted to clear the deck and sweep everything before me, but it wasn't like that. I wanted to be appreciated as a major novelist, and the book was respected, but not embraced. This was all because of Reik. He was Germanic, and had convinced me that I should be a person of stature in the world, and he was thinking of Europe, where it was possible to have that kind of career, but in America, if you insist on having it your own way, it takes a lot longer."

Around this time Maxwell accepted an invitation from Smith College to take part in a seminar on writing that included Saul Bellow and Ralph Ellison. Having decided to give up writing, he went to Pennsylvania Station and took a seat on the train to Northampton, Massachusetts, and began making notes for a speech he had agreed to deliver.

The speech begins with Maxwell's description of a Chinese scroll in the possession of the Metropolitan Museum of Art. The scroll depicts the spring festival on the river, a standard motif of Chinese painting. "It has three themes woven together:" he said, "the river, which comes down from the upper right, and the road along the river, and the people on the riverbanks. As the scroll unwinds, there is, first, some boys who cannot go to the May Day festival because they have to watch their goats. Then there is a country house, and several people starting out for the city, and a farmer letting water into a field by means of a water wheel, and then more people and buildings — all kinds of people all going toward the city for the festival. And along the riverbank there are various entertainers — a magician, a female tightrope walker, several fortunetellers, a phrenologist, a man selling spirit money, a man selling patent medicine, a storyteller."

As a writer, Maxwell said, he felt that he belonged among "the shoddy entertainers earning their living on the riverbank on May Day," because "writers — especially narrative writers — are people who perform tricks."

He described several versions of what he was talking about: "Before I came up here, I took various books down from their shelf and picked out some examples of the kind of thing I mean. Here is one:

'I have just returned this morning from a visit to my landlord — the solitary neighbor that I shall be troubled with . . .'

"One of two things — there will be more neighbors turning up than the narrator expects, or else he will very much wish that they had. And the reader is caught; he cannot go away until he finds out which of his two guesses is correct. This is, of course, a trick . . .

"Here is another trick: *'Call me Ishmael . . .'* A pair of eyes looking into your eyes. A face. A voice. You have entered into a personal relationship with a stranger, who will perhaps make demands on you, extraordinary personal demands; who will perhaps insist that you love him; who perhaps will love you in a way that is upsetting and uncomfortable . . ."

He suggested a pattern for a story: "It would help if you would give what I am now about to read to you only half your attention. It doesn't require any more than that, and if you listen only now and then, you will see better what I am driving at. Begin with breakfast and the tipping problem. Begin with the stealing of the marmalade dish and the breakfast tray still there. The marmalade dish, shaped like a shell, is put on the cabin-class breakfast tray by mistake, this once. It belongs in first class. Begin with the gate between first and second class . . ."

He discussed the working habits of a specimen writer and the complications and obstacles and setbacks and victories of his working day:

"But what, seriously, was accomplished by these writers or can the abstract dummy novelist I have been describing hope to accomplish? Not life, of course; not the real thing; not children and roses; but only a facsimile that is called literature. To achieve this facsimile the writer has, more or less, to renounce his birthright to reality, and few people have a better idea of what it is — of its rewards and satisfactions, or of what to do with a whole long day. What's in it for him? The hope of immortality? The chances are not good enough to interest a sensible person. Money? Well, money is not money anymore. Fame? For the young, who are in danger always of being ignored, of being overlooked at the party, perhaps, but no one over the age of forty who is in his right mind would want to be famous. It would interfere with his work, with his family life. Why then should the successful manipulation of illusions be everything to a writer? Why does he bother to make up stories and nov-els? If you ask him, you will probably get any number of answers, none of them straightforward. You might as well ask a sailor why it is that he has chosen to spend his life at sea."

Some time before the train arrived, he realized that he loved writing so much that he could never give it up.

Two

THERE IS no other way to begin as a writer or as anything else than by imitation. You find, by chance or design, the works or the philosophies that appeal to you and begin to make use of them. At first it appears that you are no writer (or musician or painter or lawyer) at all, but only a collection of gestures and observations other people have already made and of references to them. Gradually, the influences recede, they become absorbed, they settle into you, so that instead of being the patterns that determine how your own work sounds or looks or proceeds, they become the technical means you might make use of to describe another person's face, the workings on each other of conflicting emotions, the weather, the impression of a landscape, or the design of a strategy for solving a problem. Jimmy Garrison, who had been a member of the John Coltrane Quartet, must have found himself in need of money during the early nineteen-seventies, because he took a semester's teaching position at the college I went to, and was my faculty advisor, so I once heard him say, "First you have to learn all about your instrument, then you have to learn all about music, then you have to forget it all and learn how to play." In the forgetting one makes use of one's influences. It is important to have the best influences possible, to read the best books, listen to the best music, study the best paintings. How widely your interest spreads, how deeply, how long it continues are individual matters.

Surely the character and the abilities of the person who helps you matter also. I am as aware as anyone, I think, of how fortunate I was to have Maxwell's attention. I do not believe in false modesty — it is a form of arrogance — but I also have no idea whether the work I have done has lasting merit. There are so many other ways to have done it, so many other choices I might have made. And someone else might have handled the same material more gracefully or with more ingenuity or insight or with greater objectivity. All I could manage was what I did at the time. I know that it is much better than it would have been had I not had Maxwell read it. Even on those occasions when he had no active hand in something I wrote, the choices I made, the way I approached a subject, the order in which I told what I knew, the attitude I adopted, were determined by his example and influence. Not that I was conscious of it, any more than a tennis player has in mind as he swings his racket the person who taught him his strokes. As I was writing about the Maxwells for their memorial, I realized that my sentences sounded like his. If I were younger and he was still living, I might have been concerned that I was overtaken by his influence when I should perhaps have resisted it. Instead, I felt elated at being able to summon him, obliquely, by surrendering to the words as they came through my hands onto the page.

In writing about him, I find myself again and again using the present tense.

We worked side by side for fifteen years; it took me that long to have sufficient confidence in my own judgment not to depend on his. A different sort of man might have given me reason to doubt myself, felt competitive, lost patience.

One afternoon following another, one piece or one book succeeding another, we sat beside each other at a table — sometimes at Maxwell's apartment in New York, sometimes at the house in Westchester, and sometimes in the woods surrounding a rented house in Wellfleet — and he suggested cuts or changed a word I had learned recently to plain English, and otherwise taught me what a writer needs to know. Not that much, it turns out: when to compress and when to handle a subject at length; the order in which to present things; how to arrive at a companionable style; the benefit of the surprising juxtaposition; an awareness of what is and what isn't sensible to ask a reader to be a witness to. "Write as if you wish to be understood by an unusually bright ten-year-old," he said, or, "Henry James said 'Dramatize, dramatize, dramatize,' not 'Generalize, generalize, generalize.'" Or he took out scissors and cut up my sentences and rearranged them and pasted them back on the page. Or he leaned back from the table and asked, "Isn't there a simpler way to say that?" and I explained what I had been trying to convey, and he wrote my explanation in the margin and said, "That's it," and I was surprised to see that words I had just spoken could be writing.

I know that Maxwell and I were very different people, but we spent so much time together, and were so intimate in our conversations, and I relied so heavily on him and, without realizing it, modeled certain parts of my behavior after his, that I sometimes felt as if we were nearly alike. Proof that such thinking could be carried too far came to me some years ago in a dream in which I went to a tailor to order my writer's coat. In the logic of the dream, having such a coat was a privilege offered by a guild to an apprentice it was ready to admit. I stood in front of the tailor's mirror while he held a tape measure along my arms and down my back and across my shoulders and then told me that my coat would be ready in a week. When I picked it up, he gave me a baseball jacket made from stripes of colors arranged like a hand of cards. I told him it wasn't my coat. He said it was. I said that writers' coats are blazers made of green or brown corduroy. Maxwell had a closet of such coats.

When I gave Maxwell a manuscript, he read it to the end, before suggesting any changes, in order to see what my intentions were and whether the writing had what he called the breath of life. He had never worked with a writer handling factual material, except in the form of memoir, and he used often to say, I don't know a thing about fact writing. What brought on this remark, I think, were those parts of a piece which I had handled in a too literal way. When I began writing, I had confidence in anything that had actually happened — that is, I felt a fact earned its place in a piece because its appearance involved a depiction of reality. Later, I learned that except in the simplest and strictest forms of journalism, facts are best used judiciously, when they advance a narrative, or dramatize an element of someone's character, or contribute emotional weight to a scene. Or in the service of description when they can be employed in such a way that they illuminate an unusual or eccentric aspect of a subject and therefore reverberate poetically.

Sylvia Townsend Warner, who worked with Maxwell for nearly forty years, wrote him a letter (it is included in *The Element of Lavishness,* a book of their correspondence) that contained the following observation: "I don't thank you enough for writing so much of my stories for me. There they sit in *The New Yorker,* looking so polished and erudite. I read them, and see your hand, held out to save, in almost every paragraph. They should bear a footnote at the end: kindness of Mr. William Maxwell."

The less I knew about writing, the less I liked it when Maxwell changed something I'd written. Occasionally he would cross out a sentence, and I would grit my teeth. Sometimes I thought I would change it back when I got home, but when I got home his version always looked more apt, sleeker, or more thoughtful and refined than mine did. He treated me as a writer, not as someone whose feelings needed to be considered. I was there to learn, to receive help, and in such a circumstance the understanding is: You've let yourself in for this; here is what you need to know and do.

Usually the passages that Maxwell drew lines through were the ones I had worked hardest on and was most pleased by. I didn't yet know that they were likely, for just that reason, to be self-conscious, or whimsical, or not funny when they should have been, or simply overwritten. My complacency about them, the self-congratulation, was itself a signal of my judgment's having failed me. Maxwell was always suspicious of a manuscript a writer was excessively pleased with. The best writing came to him, he said, from writers who appeared in his doorway, looking anxious and uncertain and all but defeated, "green around the gills," he said. Writing, he wrote to Sylvia Townsend Warner, "must be done on one's hands and knees."

For a while I thought that I should broaden my vocabulary, so each day I looked up five new words and wrote them down. Crepuscular, for example. Maxwell raised his eyes from my typescript one day and said, "You sound like you've swallowed a dictionary."

I was influenced by whatever I had just read. An overused effect from a piece of magazine writing was as likely to make an impression on me as something done well in a book. I hadn't grown up a reader, or, except to have been pointed in the direction of good books, been especially well educated as one, and I wasn't equipped to tell what was worthwhile and what wasn't. My eye was nearly always attracted by the shiniest object.

What I felt when I sat beside him as he read was calm. I had done all the work that I knew how to do, and now, through his asking me what I really meant to say, or what had been the resolution of the difficulty I had left off describing before I should have, or whether I hadn't gone on too much in my reaction to something, the piece would be made better than I knew how to make it. When he was finished, I would appear to be smarter than I was and more capable. Maxwell taught me to write the way primitive fathers taught their sons to stalk, to study tracks, to observe the behavior of their prey, to watch the sky for weather, to note the bloom of the bush that signifies that the fish in their migrations have returned to the river. A cobbler teaching a young man to make shoes is what I also sometimes thought of, I suppose because the things I needed to know were so practical and primary: how to write dialogue that sounded like someone actually speaking, how to make the reader forget there was someone between him and the landscape he was reading about, how to convey the impression of a scene with some directness of effect. Vladimir Horowitz once said that he imagined himself when he played the piano as being on the other side of the notes on the page, looking out.

Editing is a matter of understanding what a writer is trying to say and helping him say it if he needs the help. It is the work of an editor to make sure that the writer means what he says and says what he means, preferably with a degree of concision. The writers Maxwell worked with were on the whole so accomplished that his position also involved taking delight in what they brought into being. He knew when something worked or didn't, or when a story's success was a matter of the magazine's tastes, and he had no difficulty identifying and describing the problem. He was straightforward if the news was bad, a kindness that pained him, but his hope was that the writer would put the matter behind him and begin another piece. When he retired, he was relieved to be no longer in the position of having to tell a writer that the magazine was unable to accept his or her manuscript. He once rejected a story by Mavis Gallant, then read it later in a book and, realizing he had been wrong, wrote her to say so.

Maxwell brought to editing, to reading another writer's work and helping him improve it, helping him see things he hadn't seen — repetitions, loquaciousness, the overuse of certain words, or the inexact use of them, a wrong turn taken, or the failure to bring a piece to its best conclusion — a selflessness that I never saw an example of anywhere else. If he thought you had something correct, he took pleasure in it. Reading was a near spiritual hunger with him, and he spent the last few years of his life reading hours a day, going back over the books he had loved. When I was having difficulty beginning my second book, he said, "Why don't you write me a letter each morning with the material you were intending to work on, then mail it to me." After several months I retrieved the letters and found that they formed a draft.

His advice was erudite and penetrating and completely reliable and uncontaminated by competition. He was known to see in stories writers had given up on the possibilities for development of a character or a line of narrative or for compressing a scene or combining one scene with another or for moving several sentences or a paragraph from the beginning of a piece to nearer the end so that the emotional tone of the story was changed, and the story brought to life and made resonant in a way that it hadn't been. Partly this is a matter of imagination, of receptivity, a capacity for seeing others the way they would like to be seen, of a selfless interest in encouraging talent, and an intimacy with the catalog of technical possibility. What suggestions he made he offered unobtrusively, and he qualified them by saying that if the writer didn't agree with them, he should overlook them. As to how other writers regarded his opinion, when J. D. Salinger finished *The Catcher in the Rye*, he drove to the Maxwells' house and over the course of an afternoon read it to them on their porch.

*

In the way that a baseball player might regard himself as a participant in a tradition involving Gehrig and Ruth, Maxwell thought himself engaged as a writer in an occupation that goes back to the blind old man at the crossroads — the professional storyteller, led around by a boy, addressing whoever will listen and using his skill to hold the attention of his audience as the light fades and everyone has a good reason for going home. Somewhat subversively, he believed that the patterns of ordinary life, acutely observed, provide more drama and structure and emotional resonance than purely imagined events are likely to. This is not the same as suggesting that a writer's imagination ought to surrender itself to the outward pattern of actual happenings; only that in describing the past we are involved in a never-ending process of self-deception, and that we cannot present any version of the facts that is not at least partly invention.

Between 1934 and 1994, Maxwell published six novels, two volumes of stories, a book of literary improvisations somewhat in the style of fables, a book of essays, a family history, two children's books, and an edition of collected stories. The fables, in *The Old Man at the Railroad Crossing,* are imaginary and were mostly written for occasions in his family — his wife's birthday or at Christmas to be found hanging from the tree by one of his daughters. He wrote them by sitting at his typewriter in an attitude of receptivity until something was handed to him, as if from his unconscious. Often it was the phrase "Once upon a time . . ." and from that everything else followed. "A person I didn't know anything about," he writes in the book's introduction, "and had never known in real life — a man who had no enemies, a girl who doesn't know whether to listen to her heart or her mind, a woman who never draws a breath except to complain, an old man afraid of falling — stepped from the wings and began to act out something I must not interrupt or interfere with, but only be a witness to: a life, with the fleeting illuminations that anybody's life offers, written in sand with a pointed stick and erased by the next high tide." The only one of his novels that is almost entirely imagined is *Time Will Darken It,* which unfolded as a series of conversations among his characters. As he began a chapter, he determined what character had not spoken to another in a while and put down what each had to tell the other.

An autobiographical writer is often trying to deliver himself from an experience that haunts him. In several stories and two novels Maxwell handled the death of his mother. As far as his novels are concerned, he did it first in *They Came Like Swallows,* published in 1937, and again in *So Long, See You Tomorrow,* published in 1980. In the first book he writes about the experience directly; in the second his way of treating it is more oblique, what he is writing about really is his mother's absence from the family and the permanent shadow such deprivation cast over the household. The consequences of her death are combined with the description and aftermath of the murder of a tenant farmer by the husband of a woman he had fallen in love with. The love affair that led to the murder and the effect of the killing on the life of the boy who lost his mother, Maxwell allowed himself to imagine. The facts were no longer retrievable.

They Came Like Swallows is included in the Modern Library, and in the introduction Maxwell wrote: "Because I was only ten at the time of my mother's death, there were things I didn't know or that were kept from me. I think that in the end I got all the circumstances right. But I am not sure that these later retellings are as affecting as the first one, where I made myself two years younger than I actually was, played ducks and drakes with chronology, gave one person's experience to another, introduced domestic habits from households I came to know later, and freely mixed fact with fiction. It may be simply that when I was writing *They Came Like Swallows* the heartbreaking actual events had not yet receded into the past.

"It took all winter to finish Part Two. I wrote Part Three in ten days. Much of the time I walked the floor, framing sentences in my mind and then brushing the tears away with my hand so I could see the typewriter keys. I was weeping, I think, both for what happened — for I could not write about my mother's death without reliving it — and for events that took place only in my imagination. I don't suppose that I was entirely sane."

In presenting to Maxwell in 1993 the Gold Medal for Fiction of the American Academy of Arts and Letters — that body's highest award, which is given every six years — Joseph Mitchell said, "William Maxwell's principal theme, like James Joyce's, is the sadness that often exists at the heart of a family . . . He is as aware as any novelist who ever lived of what human beings are capable of." Maxwell's stories and novels are meticulously crafted. Even so, the finished work is without any self-consciousness or sign of effort. There are no arabesques. Mitchell also said, "Nevertheless, in his pages one often reads with surprise descriptions and observations that seem truer and more revealing and more powerful and more memorable and more shocking than the deliberately shocking scenes and observations found in the pages of many of his contemporaries."

Once, when Maxwell was in his eighties, we were riding in a taxi and he said, "Whenever I write a sentence now I ask myself, Is this true?" If he found a sentence he liked in a paragraph he had no use for, he took scissors, cut out the sentence, and put it in a folder until he could find a place for it. As he got older, he said, his work consisted more and more of such sentences, which was also the reason it grew shorter.

When he worked on a novel, he liked to hold an image in mind as a metaphor for the book's design. A stone thrown into a pond, sending ripples over the surface of the water, and then a second stone thrown and a third, until the ripples merged and gravity restored the stillness of the surface (*Time Will Darken It*). Or mountains in the distance across a plain toward which the reader made his way, a chapter at a time (*The Folded Leaf*). He believed that writing ought to advance sentence by sentence, not paragraph by paragraph or page by page, and that every word should carry weight. He would tell me, when I struggled against some emotional obstacle, that the writer and the critic couldn't occupy the room at the same time. *The New Yorker,* when I arrived in 1980, had a house philosophy that writing was arduous and draining and next thing to impossible, which was an oppressive atmosphere for a young man. The place seemed a peerage of gloomy old men. Once at a party I heard a woman say to Maxwell, "Oh, you're a writer. What a terrible, lonely life," and he brought her up short by saying, "There's nothing I love to do more." For me the remark was liberating, and I have felt ever since that writing, even at its most difficult, is a privilege. He believed that while working on a piece of writing, a writer should hold nothing back. Everything you have is never more than enough for the purpose at hand. When he couldn't decide which way a story should proceed, he followed all the possibilities until it became clear which was best.

When he was young he liked writing that was poetic and intricate such as Virginia Woolf's prose, but as he got older he was drawn more toward writing that resembled a writer's habitual patterns of speech and that was simple and to the point. He was fond of a remark by the critic John Hall Wheelock that writing involves the imposition of a line of words on a line of feeling.

After Maxwell died, I read his copy of *Autobiographies* by William Butler Yeats, because I knew he was fond of it. I had borrowed many books from him over the years, but I had never found any notations in them, so it was a surprise to find that he had drawn a line in pencil next to this paragraph: "We should write out our own thoughts in as nearly as possible the language we thought them in, as though in a letter to an intimate friend. We should not disguise them in any way; for our lives give them force as the lives of people in plays give force to their words. Personal utterance, which had almost ceased in English literature, could be as fine an escape from rhetoric and abstraction as drama itself. But my father would hear of nothing but drama; personal utterance was only egotism. I knew it was not, but as yet did not know how to explain the difference. I tried from then on to write out of my emotions exactly as they came to me in life, not changing them to make them more beautiful. 'If I can be sincere and make my language natural, and without becoming discursive, like a novelist, and so indiscreet and prosaic,' I said to myself, 'I shall, if good luck or bad luck make my life interesting, be a great poet; for it will be no longer a matter of literature at all.' Yet when I re-read those early poems which gave me so much trouble, I find little but romantic convention, unconscious drama. It is so many years before one can believe enough in what one feels even to know what the feeling is."

When he was getting close to ninety, Maxwell said that he no longer had the inclination for sustained literary effort, for holding the pattern of a story or a novel in mind for the time it would take to complete it. He sometimes said that he seemed to have lost touch with the place where stories and novels come from. He still loved, he said, to write sentences. In the last few years of his life he wrote introductions to books by Maeve Brennan and Joseph Mitchell and for my book about being a policeman, which was being brought back into print; an essay about the approach of his ninetieth birthday; the introduction to *They Came Like Swallows;* and an essay describing two old men, Austin Strong, whose grandmother married Robert Louis Stevenson, and Rodman Gilder, a playwright, both of whom he knew when he was in his forties. His disengagement from the source of his work was not something he felt reconciled to. He sometimes said that when people asked him what he was writing, even though he knew they only meant to be polite, he wanted to pick up something and throw it at them.

Maxwell wrote about Austin Strong and Rodman Gilder to mark the occasion of his ninetieth birthday and his fifty years as a member of the club he belonged to in Manhattan, and he read what he had written at a dinner held at the club in his honor. Although attendance was limited to members of the club and their guests, nearly five hundred people turned up to hear him, several hundred more than the club had expected. Strong and Gilder were each a generation older than Maxwell, and in describing the end of their lives, he wrote:

"The following winter when Austin did not appear at the club for a week or so I inquired of the doorman about him and was told that he had been unwell but was better and that Mrs. Strong had said visitors would be welcome. I went looking for Rodman, who said soberly, 'Heart attack.' When I was led upstairs to Austin's bedroom I found him sitting up in a four-poster. Except for his poor color he was his usual self. He said he would be back in the club soon. Instead, I found myself attending his funeral."

The directness with which Maxwell said this, near as he seemed at ninety to his own funeral, made many people draw in their breath quickly.

"Shortly after that," he went on, "Rodman sat back in his chair, with one arm behind his head to think about something, and never finished the thought. That made two funerals. I said, I will never again love an old man. They die on you."

I had persuaded myself that he would not do this to me.

Three

My FATHER was forty-two when I was born, and the men and women who occasionally came to our house were of his and my mother's generation, and too old or too remote to appeal to me. If I was introduced to any of them, I was brought to a halt and presented with someone whose bearing was formal and who towered over me and perhaps shook my hand. The only face I recall being intrigued by was Maxwell's, because I was aware of a warmth within it, through his eyes, I suppose, or something appealing in the softness of his voice.

By the time I was born whatever interest my father had in being a father, he had shed. If I try to reconstruct the atmosphere of my childhood, I come up with scenes that are probably imaginary more than factual but that have a degree of truthfulness nonetheless. My father's back receding from me is one of them. On his way to the barn, or out the door to the train station. What I might do to divert him, to hold his attention, to keep him in the room, I had no idea.

What did I want him to be? Someone who made me feel protected, safe from whatever threatened me. A man who knew valuable things, the answers to mysteries, what to do when you feel terribly sad or are afraid. Who took my existence seriously. The yearning in the mind of a boy for his father is sufficiently common that I think it can be taken for granted.

When I became acquainted through a picture book with the story of the Labyrinth, I felt that I recognized the figure of the Minotaur. My father had wide shoulders and strong arms, and although he was not tall, he was to a child — he seemed to stand between me and the sky, as if his face were up in the branches of the trees — and the way that he moved conveyed an impression, not exactly of menace, but at least of animal force only half suppressed. He did not lose his temper often, but he lost it suddenly and enigmatically; that is, one couldn't be sure that something that made him angry once would make him angry again, or whether its opposite would, which left me uncertain about how to approach him, and keeping to the living room if he was in the kitchen or my bedroom if he was in the living room. His manner was brusque, and he was always surprised when something hurtful he did had consequences. When he behaved thoughtlessly, he expected to be forgiven. This was the result, I think, of his inability to imagine himself in someone else's position, to regard another person's life sympathetically. He was too impatient to make the effort, or too inattentive, or too much of an extrovert, or simply lacked the talent for it.

My three brothers are enough older than I am that I didn't really grow up among them. My oldest brother was enrolled in boarding school the year after I was born, and before long the others were, too. The house they left me behind in was not peaceful. My mother drank secretly. My father carried on affairs in the city, during lunch hours or on afternoons when he could invent a reason to be away from his office. When he came home in the evening, my mother would make spiteful remarks, until one of them struck home and a fight began. Of course she bore only half the blame. Even a fraught marriage is sustained by an intricate series of agreements. Having her drunk and going to bed early was what my father intended, whether he realized it or not. Being married to a woman who appeared unable to hold up her end of the arrangement made him seem to be put upon, and his life as a philanderer easier to justify: through no fault of my own, my marriage is a wreck, I am entitled to find comfort where I can. The drinking disabled her and protected him from remorse.

I suppose that when he and Maxwell were introduced to each other on the train platform, they shook hands. I suppose my father went home and said that he had met the man who lived in the cabin down the hill and who could sometimes be seen from the road on his knees in a flower garden. Perhaps he called and offered Maxwell a ride to the station. Anyway, they rode together for twenty years, deeply content in each other's company, accepting of each other's natures. Jung says somewhere that the elements of a person's unconscious life that remain in the shadows tend to assert themselves in such a way that the events they influence appear to be the workings of fate. As a child, I absorbed impressions of Maxwell, of his aptness for being an alternative to my father, a man who appeared to be kinder and more responsive, more thoughtful, and whose company was less turbulent. I responded to his gentleness; his eyes would fall on a person like a kind of light and were expressive of calmness and affection. As I got older I noted the figure he cut, and in searching for a model of how to be in the world, the way young men do, I found his example worth emulating. He was comfortable in his manner, and he never labored for an effect. There was no mark upon him of anxiety or of coarseness.

Because I was afraid of my father, I was drawn to someone who was his opposite. In my twenties and early thirties, I thought that my friendship with Maxwell involved merely the unfolding of a worldly process: my father loved him, and somehow I knew I would arrive at an age when he would also be my friend, as if the friendship were a legacy I would come into.

When I was a child I used to wake early. Around the corner of the living room doorway I would see my father, at the far end of the room, reading a book by the light that came through the window or, in the winter, from a lamp on the table beside him. I knew he was not to be disturbed. When I was older I learned that he had been susceptible to headaches and to unbidden apprehensions — in the city, he was afraid to walk past an open window for fear that he might throw himself out of it — and that his means of trying to come to terms with such turmoil was to take up Christian Science. He was reading Mary Baker Eddy. Rising early like a monk. Looking for guidance. The behavior was so at odds with his nature, which was forceful and resistant to contemplation, that it can only indicate the extent to which he felt that the control of his life was slipping through his hands.

Reconciliation is important as one gets older. Holding on to resentments is corrosive. I think that I had a fortunate childhood, but I would change some things about it if I could. What I saw as grievances I now regard as circumstances I would have preferred to be different.

Defeated and unhappy is how I now view my father. Combative when there was no reason to be. Restless, unable to enjoy his sons or his wife. An incorrigible skirt-chaser. None of it can have been sustaining. My father's physical roughness was appealing to me. He was strong and vital and spent nearly all of his time outdoors and conveyed to me the impression that work done with one's hands is honorable. When he threw his skates and a hockey stick in the back of the car and drove to one of the frozen ponds, he took me with him. Maxwell was no athlete of any kind. If he had been the one to give me my existence, his love of the imaginative life, his sensitivity, might have been confusing for me, too exotic. Inaccessible, at least. Confirmation of this, I think, came in the form of my always having kept a certain part of my nature under wraps when I was around the Maxwells. I am more like my father than I am comfortable admitting. I was much louder than either of the Maxwells was or any of their friends I ever met. I was sometimes crude in my antagonisms. My opinions might be based on jealousies. I wasn't refined. I had read only a few of the books that Maxwell had read, and I doubt I could have discussed them knowledgeably — not that he liked especially to talk about books, but I think he might have with his closest friends who were writers. I have in mind Francis Steegmuller and Frank O'Connor and Robert Fitzgerald, whose learning and sophistication Maxwell admired when they were at Harvard together.

It has occurred to me that if Maxwell had been my father, I might have found the quiet of the household stultifying, and my parents' romance and their preoccupation with art and literature impenetrable, and later on I might have sought out the man I remembered from my childhood who lived up the road — the Sunday painter with the tools in his barn, who, when the snow was deep enough, hitched his horses to a carriage sled and drove over the fields, and who seemed ebullient and mischievous and full of an appetite for life. Perhaps it was naïve of me to expect that the means of addressing the moral complications of life could all be found in the example of one man and woman.

My father won some awards in high school for paintings he had made — reproductions, I think they were — and instead of college he went to an art school in New York City. The school's quarters were too small for all the students to occupy the premises at once, so half of them spent the morning at a museum, drawing, and in the afternoon changed places with the ones who had spent the morning in the classrooms and studios. I don't think my father intended to be a painter; I don't think his nature included a sufficient supply of the nerve or the devotion or the quality of attention such a life requires if one is to face down all the hardships and disappointments and indifference involved. What I believe he might have wanted to be was an illustrator, but living constantly on the resources of his imagination wouldn't have suited him, either. Too high strung is what he probably was. Also, too gregarious for a solitary life. I don't think it is a coincidence that he ended up a magazine art director, with the power to hire illustrators and photographers and to accept or dismiss their work, and the satisfaction of knowing that some of them were financially dependent on his approval. He liked having the opportunity to pass judgment. I never heard that he exercised it unfairly. I know that he supported at least one photographer who had difficulty finding work elsewhere. He paid artists when he accepted their work, when the custom was to pay on publication. The authority of his position consoled him, I think, for not having the resolve to live an artist's life. A creative life of any kind would have required him to have a congenial relationship with whatever intimations arose from the deeper layers of his being; instead, he was in some way resentful of impulses from the unconscious, of the feminine. Part of his nature was insufficiently enlarged, and by influencing the fortunes of people who led such lives, by judging their work and seeing to their welfare, he was able to feel superior to them and at the same time regard himself as benevolent.

Writing is a form of truth telling, and it sometimes involves the defeat of one's personality. The wish to be liked. The occasional lack of nerve. The self-consciousness, self-deception, and self-congratulation. The regard for proprieties. Our personalities might be thought of as the gestures, manners, attitudes, and ways of behaving we enact in order to keep other people from knowing what we really are thinking. A great deal of our time we spend looking inward. Behind any matter-of-fact, transparent, busy, ordinary life is a territory marked by regrets, daydreams, memories, secrets, and hidden places of withdrawal. It is difficult to make the outer life and the inner life converge, to conduct ourselves truthfully, which is different from saying wounding things to others and congratulating ourselves for cultivating the virtue of candor.

I think of the writer Harold Brodkey, who as a young man was a neighbor of my parents; he married a woman who grew up on the road they and the Maxwells lived on. I knew him in my childhood; his daughter and I played together; and then I didn't see him for twenty years, by which time we were colleagues at *The New Yorker*. The first thing he said to me then was "The thing about your father was that he couldn't stand being second-rate." He didn't mean that my father would tolerate nothing except being the best. He meant that my father was the art director of a trivial magazine and not a painter of some stature, and that he resented it. I loved my father and was stung by Brodkey's remark, although I knew it was partially true — that my father felt inferior in the company of people who were, what? Braver? Less conventional? Less inhibited? I'm not sure. I also knew that Brodkey intended to disturb me. I told Maxwell, to whom Brodkey had dedicated his first book, what Brodkey's estimate of my father had been and Maxwell said, "Didn't you know that Harold's father drove a junk wagon?"

One wheel turning inside another is what it put me in mind of, and a smaller one inside that one, and so on.

I never asked Maxwell why he took me on, but of course it had something to do with his affection for my father and for his not having a son. And I arrived in his life at a time when his daughters were establishing themselves in lives that were independent of their parents' influence. That I showed up while they were in the midst of it and would hear nothing said against Maxwell or his wife only made it more difficult for them.

I am not in a position to say whether he saw any talent in me. I don't know that I have that much. I know I work hard. I know Maxwell took note of that. All he ever said on the matter, to me anyway, was that I was a quick study, which is something I had heard before — that is, he felt that once he had pointed out a questionable passage to me, I tended not to repeat the mistake. I made different mistakes. And I don't know that it is the highest praise. Certainly I was persistent. I would call every few weeks with the pages I had written. He was unquestionably the most important American editor of short fiction during the twentieth century, and most writers probably thought that having once had his attention they shouldn't ask for more. Since I was not a literary person, I was protected by not being fully aware of his stature as either a writer or an editor. By the time I began to be paid for my writing, I knew who William Shawn was. I was twenty-four when I started writing and twenty-eight when I went to work for *The New Yorker*, and too intimidated in Shawn's presence to say much. Writing for him never came easily to me. I was too much put in mind of the other writers he had dealt with, of what he had read over the years. I viewed Maxwell as my father's friend and did not consider my asking the favor of his attention was more than was reasonable and didn't think of the writers he had given it to before or whether I could make a case for having my name raised among theirs.

He would sometimes say to me, "There are a lot of ways to make a living," which annoyed me. I didn't know if he meant that he didn't believe I had the talent to keep going in the face of the discouragement I'd received, or was trying to give me an honorable way out if I thought I needed one. Still, it bruised my feelings. And made me resolve to work harder. What I wanted was for him to be proud of me.

Did he ever disappoint me? Twice that I can remember. The first occasion was of no consequence, a favor that he wasn't willing to satisfy and that he later satisfied for someone else, going to far more trouble than my request involved and for someone I thought he had less reason to be helpful to. As I look at it now, he did so many favors for me, and had very few occasions to do them for this other friend. Or perhaps he found it easier to say no to me, assuming that I would understand.

The second time occurred during the period when my first marriage was foundering. One afternoon Maxwell and I were having lunch, and I took a deep breath and told him that I was drawn toward a woman I had met a year earlier (and who, several years later, became my wife). I said that I had stepped off the elevator one day at my office, and she was waiting to get on. I recognized her as someone who had begun working at the magazine a few weeks earlier. Before my mind focused, I thought, She is going to make someone a terrific wife. I went into my office and closed the door and resolved that if I was ever in a room and she came into it, I would leave. It was clear that my wife and I had a troubled marriage, and I was determined not to threaten it. I believed that if I just denied everything I was feeling, I would be able eventually to make things work. It was a matter of discipline.

For a year, more or less, I left the room. Then I began not leaving the room. I had never engaged in an infidelity but I wanted to. I didn't want to be married anymore. I told Maxwell all of this in the hope that he would tell me what to do, how to proceed, how to recover myself, and he said, "I have never been unfaithful to Emmy." Did he mean, I have never had the feelings you are having, and so cannot help you? Did he mean, Sorry you're having difficulty, but my own conduct has been impeccable, so you're on your own. Did he mean, Instead of considering your difficulty, I'd prefer to reflect on my own unblemished character. That he preferred not to get involved? That he disapproved? He had friends who had divorced and married again under similar circumstances, sometimes more than twice, and he had never said anything against them or their characters or seen less of them. I knew only that I had asked for help and that he had refused to consider the matter.

The only subject I was aware of that made both him and his wife uncomfortable was criticism of my mother or father. If I said something against the way I had been raised, Maxwell tended to repeat a remark my mother had made about me: "This is my last one," she said, "and I'm going to enjoy him." Such an observation has a multiplicity of associations, not all of them benign, but he intended that it stand as proof that she had been devoted to me, and that I was being not exactly ungrateful in return, but at least unmindful of evidence that seemed to undermine my right to hold grievances.

After my first book was published I had dinner with the Maxwells and my parents. My mother thanked Maxwell for all he had done for me, and he said, "It is something to have a son delivered to you." What I would have expected him to accept also was that such a relationship between us would not have been possible had I been content with my father.

It took years before it was borne in on me that Maxwell's remarks were defensive. My father once told me that when he was having lunch with Maxwell at the club they belonged to in New York, Maxwell, describing the way his daughters had found it necessary to withdraw themselves to assert their independence, had begun to weep. Any criticism I made of my mother and father raised the question of how the Maxwells might have brought up their daughters differently and to what extent the responsibility for the estrangement and the resentment the girls were expressing was theirs.

Once I realized this, I added a preface to remarks about my parents, saying that they had behaved in the manner of the people they were and made decisions they thought were correct, and instead of repeating my mother's remark, Maxwell would say, "We cannot choose our parents." Which, even so, implied a state of resignation I usually felt too agitated to embody.

Maxwell's career as a novelist separated him, intentionally, from *The New Yorker*. He had no ambition for a title or for authority and did not pursue either of them when he could have. When William Shawn told him that if he wanted to be considered for the position of head fiction editor they should talk, Maxwell said he wasn't interested. He knew that the job would require his being in the office every day, and that would mean the end of his writing. His books gave him an independence from the magazine. No matter what took place in the office, he had an alternate life. He always told me to keep some piece of writing to the side, something that the magazine couldn't touch and would make my opinion of my work not dependent on its response.

The trait that comes to my mind more often than any other, when I recall him, is his fierceness. It was derived, I suppose, from the settlers and country people in back of him. I didn't think of it often when he was alive, because he concealed it so artfully. He was neither confrontational nor combative. Only immovable. Resolute. When he disagreed with an editor's suggestion, he tended to say nothing, to bring the work to a halt, until the editor relented. I once told him about changes that an editor was trying to impose on something I had written and how I felt I had no choice but to accept them, and he said, "Just say, 'I don't like it.'" What he meant was, Don't insist on telling the editor what little regard you have for his judgment, don't insult him, don't be arrogant or defensive, don't act in a way that is patently insubordinate, don't become deflected from the objective. Simply tell him the truth. The editor was unlikely to answer, I don't care whether you like it or not, that's beside the point, and so on.

My relationship with one of the editors I worked for was especially fraught with complications. Maxwell told me to pretend each time I was in the editor's presence that I was meeting him for the first time. It didn't entirely answer, but it meant that every time I was in his company I did not refer to the catalog of resentments I bore against him. It gave me a little room to breathe.

When someone asked Maxwell about a person he didn't care for, he would say something such as, So-and-so is a wonder, isn't he? And leave it at that. If he was certain that the person he was talking to was discreet, he might say, The less said about him or her, the better. When he was in his sixties he was interviewed by a newspaper journalist who quoted his remarks ineptly. After that, any interviewer who came to see him took a seat in his study, asked a question, and Maxwell wrote his reply on his typewriter. He then turned the typewriter around so that the interviewer could read the reply. If there was a related question, Maxwell typed his answer on the same sheet of paper. If the next question had nothing to do with the one before it, he rolled a new sheet of paper into the carriage. The interviewer left with a file of papers, believing Maxwell's behavior to be an expression of courtliness.

I don't know what made him so fierce. He was often thought by people who didn't know him well to be mild-mannered. Someone who is mild-mannered, or easily pleased, doesn't work as hard as he did over the years. Such discipline has a cost, and he knew it. His schedule imposed a design on the lives of his wife and his daughters and made the household subject to his intentions. "It caused us to miss a lot of picnics," Mrs. Maxwell once told me.

I have heard people say that Maxwell's flintiness was evidence of a coldness they considered typically Midwestern, where extreme displeasure, even contempt, might be expressed by raised eyebrows or the turning away from a subject with a mild dismissal, the display of small gestures to be read for their severity. I never knew him to be unreasonably cold. Never showing one's displeasure, following through on things one has agreed to even if one no longer has the appetite for them, a sense of resignation, a tolerance for hardship, a dignity in bearing one's lot, are traits I associate with the Midwestern character of the late nineteenth century, the one that formed the personalities of the men and women Maxwell grew up among. Also an intention to behave properly. When he was in his fifties, Maxwell wrote letters to every person he felt he had harmed, to apologize.

It turned out that no one remembered the offense or recalled the incident in the same light that he did.

MY FATHER told Maxwell that I had been working at night, and he said, "Very professional." I had been working at night because I thought that what I wrote at night was more interesting than what I wrote during the day. I was afraid that what I wrote during the day sounded ordinary. To keep from feeling tired, I took a stimulant I no longer remember the name of, but that was an ingredient of a medication for bronchitis, which I had to ask the pharmacist for. I would cough and shake my head and say wasn't it my own terrible luck that I just couldn't get shed of this congestion, must be the damp winter we're having, I guess I need some of that bronchitis medicine, what's it called again, right, that's it. I began working after dinner and worked until eleven or twelve, and then I usually went to visit a friend who was the caretaker of an inn that was closed during the winter. He'd open the bar, and we'd sit, wearing our coats and sometimes seeing our breath in the air before us, and watch television. Or we'd smoke pot in his bedroom and listen to records, and by two or three I'd be tired enough to go to bed. I carried on in this fashion for about three months, and then I gave it up.

The first time I showed work to Maxwell, I took it to him at a house the Maxwells had rented in the Wellfleet woods. He read what I brought while I sat beside him. He said it looked as though I had worked hard on the sentences, and I had, insofar as I knew how. When he finished, he told me that he thought it was good and that I should keep going. He and Mrs. Maxwell left Wellfleet a few days later.

A week after that, I got a letter in which he enclosed a pamphlet called *The Writer as Illusionist* — the speech he had given at Smith College. On the flyleaf he wrote, "If you ever want me to read anything else, I would be happy to." The next time I had something to show him, I drove to New York, intending to stay overnight at the Maxwells' apartment, but I ended up getting sick and staying several days in their front bedroom. One afternoon Maxwell came home with books he had bought for me. *Berlin Stories*, by Christopher Isherwood; *Anna Karenina*; *A Sport and a Pastime*, by James Salter; Robert Fitzgerald's translation of *The Odyssey*; *A Passage to India*; *The Sudden View*, by Sybille Bedford; *The Autobiography of Benjamin Franklin*; *Memento Mori*, by Muriel Spark; *My Mortal Enemy*, by Willa Cather; and a collection of Chekhov's writings. Eventually, I read all of them except *The Odyssey*, because whenever I tried it was impenetrable to me.

A few weeks before Maxwell died I saw it on my bookshelf. I called and asked if he liked it still. "I'm mad about it," he said. "It's a kind of a fairy story. It's so lyrical, and the world is so young, full of monsters and escapes, especially Odysseus's homecoming. If you heard

Robert Fitzgerald read the homecoming, it made your hair stand up on your head." So I tried again, and learned what many people would already have known, which is that Mentor and Odysseus were comrades. Mentor is older than Odysseus, and when Odysseus leaves for Troy he asks Mentor to look after his slaves and his household, which includes his son, Telemachus. Athena occasionally inhabits Mentor, mostly to help him fortify Telemachus when he worries that he isn't up to facing an obstacle or a challenge. When Odysseus and Telemachus arrive home to take back their household from the suitors who have overrun it, Athena inhabits Mentor and makes him a warrior.

The relationship between Mentor and Telemachus suggests that in a classic arrangement of this kind the guardian not be simply a teacher or an advisor acquainting a young man or woman with the rudiments of a trade or a code of behavior, but that there also be an attachment between them. Also that the experience and the emotional maturity of the older person makes him or her a fit example for the younger one. Also that the exchange be cleansed of vanity, and that the concern of the older man or woman for the younger one is selfless.

There are all sorts of ways for such a relationship to go off the rails, I suppose. The tastes and experience and character and advice of the older person might not be worth following. The younger person might be preyed on sexually. An older person might choose a duplicitous younger one and end up being ridiculed, or cast aside for a more powerful mentor, or have his advice used against him by an avid young person intent on advancing himself. The older person might fear that the younger one will overtake him professionally and then undermine him. The older person might require a dependence from the younger one that impedes his or her maturing. Or cast a shadow the younger person feels unable to step clear of.

None of these things happened to me. When it came time to emerge from Maxwell's influence and teaching, we became friends. Such a relationship is not much different from others in our lives. Some attraction or circumstance draws two people toward each other, chance or desire, and they find themselves enlarged or they don't. What seems to hold people together through difficult periods is the awareness always that some other outcome is possible between them. Some path out of despair or indifference or being bored or frightened. I always knew with Maxwell that whatever engagement I had with him, I never got to the bottom of him. Certain of his opinions and feelings were fixed, were matters of temperament or firm belief, but many weren't. I felt even up to the last days of his life that he was refining his impressions. I talked to him over the years far more often than I should have about my problems. That is, I might have behaved with more dignity than to call him whenever I had a grievance. He never put me off. I plagued him with my troubles because I expected him (unrealistically) to cure them. Mrs. Maxwell was beautiful and rich and accomplished, and Maxwell was a great artist. I am not the only person who offered himself for adoption. I idealized them both and was of course trying to get from them the attention I had never got from my parents. Toward the end of his life Maxwell said, "The best thing I can do for you is listen," and I felt comforted.

Nietzsche somewhere remarks that when one hasn't had a good father, it is necessary to invent him. It is perhaps also true that someone who has a good father doesn't probably look for someone to replace him. Throughout mythology and folklore, a figure such as Mentor appears only in the absence of a strong father. There is no need of him otherwise. I derived my identity from Maxwell. I did not want to be like my father, but I didn't know that, except obscurely. I was drawn instead to someone who was as different from him as anyone I knew. I wanted to replace the influences and even the experiences of my childhood with something more sympathetic. Mentor is engaged in helping Telemachus find his father, who is brave and generous and compassionate and fierce, because by finding him, Telemachus will recognize the strength within himself. That Athena takes the form of a man who has been a warrior seems to me pointed. It implies a completeness of the human experience, a balance. Maxwell struck me as containing that kind of harmony.

He once said, "You are my most intimate friend," but I knew what he meant was that he had outlived the others, Robert Fitzgerald and Frank O'Connor and Francis Steegmuller especially.

What he meant was, You are my most intimate friend left.

At various stages I thought of him as my father, as a godfather, and finally as my friend. All human experience has a shared element, and especially love in any form. What I am describing is, in one version or another, common to everyone's experience.

There were two questions I couldn't ask him: Was he proud of me? And what would I do without him?

About fifteen years ago, in order to arrive at some understanding of my growing up, I occupied once or twice a week a leather chair in the office of a Jungian analyst in the Village, and after a few years of talking about other subjects, I began to wonder how I would feel when my father died. I had once considered myself close to him, but had come to believe that we weren't well suited to each other and that I had concerns and grievances I wasn't sure how to take up with him — if I could take them up at all, since by then he was elderly. It seemed unreasonable to hold him to account for the way he had behaved thirty years earlier, and if he said he regretted it, what difference would it make. Except in memory, I couldn't recover my childhood, and certainly I could change nothing that had happened; I could only change how I regarded it. Moreover, my relations with him were, after all, what had left me open to an intimate friendship with someone of his generation, and if he had done nothing else than make a close friend of Maxwell and allow me to transfer my feelings for him to his friend, he had set up a way of my being looked after.

When Maxwell was elderly, he once told me, "Of all my friends, as I look back on it, your father had the truest heart." The charming, amiable, and eccentric man who delighted Maxwell and whose friendship toward him was unstinting, was not the aloof and temperamental man I knew as my father. What I ended up feeling toward my father is sadness for the relationship I wish we had had. We had failed to make some fundamental connection when we should have, and after that, nothing that should have happened between a father and his child had gone right. Which is to say that when he died, in 1995, I missed him, but I didn't feel shipwrecked or even much thrown. What I began to be apprehensive about then was how I would feel when Maxwell died.

I often wonder what it is like to be very old. To outlive one's friends. The world one was raised in. To feel that one's relation to the world has been altered by the experiences one has collected, the person one has made one's self into, now that one's evolution is nearly complete. Also, to live at close hand with an awareness of one's death. My experience of old age consists of observing my father and mother and Maxwell advance. Since Maxwell seemed undiminished, I have the impression that a person can enrich and enlarge himself until he runs out of time. A life of the mind seems essential. Of course Maxwell was never distracted for long periods by pain or a wasting illness, but Mrs. Maxwell was, yet she preserved herself; that is, she didn't become subordinate to the course of her disease. She was never defeated. Great courage is clearly required, and resourcefulness. Brooding on the subject puts me in mind of the way young men used to wonder how they would comport themselves in combat. I wonder how I will do if I live long enough, but I have been provided with an example. I will know the standard I am falling short of. I don't mean that I believe one should be expected to summon more resources than one can manage, but the alternative — waiting to die, waking each morning and wishing one hadn't opened one's eyes, out of resignation or defeat or lack of nerve — is not an existence I hope to enact.

So far as I can tell, the processes of memory involve two stages, the first being the accumulation of images and experiences from the period before one has the use of words, when the world is mysterious and cannot be categorized, at least not extensively so. These seem to be forgotten or submerged or replaced by memories that are made fast like photographs, by means of the formal understanding of the world that arrives with being able to attach names to people and places, and words to some of the things that are happening to us. Maxwell thought he had forgotten much less of his childhood than most people do. "I don't seem to have amnesia much," he said. "It's sort of abnormal." I once said to him that I didn't think that most people remember much of their lives before the age of four or five, and he said, "It's intentional, to protect them in cases where people died or something else terrible happened. I can remember my mother's pleasure in standing me up in the bath between her legs. How old could I have been then?"

He believed that his memory would retain what he needed for his writing, so he didn't keep a journal. What he considered more promising as material was not so much what one remembered as what one couldn't forget. In middle age, he sometimes sat by himself on the commuter train and made entries for stories and novels in a notebook, more as a way of making use of the time; at least I am not aware that he ever elaborated on the sketches he composed. Sometimes, between periods of longer work, he sat at his typewriter and wrote down what came to his mind, a form of archeology. On one of these occasions, laying out material that became useful in another form, as the emotional peak of *Ancestors*, he began by describing his father's recalling an event involving Maxwell and his older brother that had been submerged in his memory for decades.

"I was brought up to believe that my father never laid his hand on me. 'Happy, yes,' he used to say. 'He was full of the Old Ned. But you were very different. There was no need to punish you.' I took his word for it and felt somehow underprivileged. This statement was not true, though it is what he sincerely believed. In the last year of his very long life he was presented with something from the underground vaults: a Sunday morning in the year 1911. I was three years old. My mother had dressed me all in white to go to dinner at my grandfather's house, and as we were crossing the street, my father saw me heading straight for a mud puddle and said, 'Bill, if you walk through that mud puddle, I'll take you upstairs and spank you.' I did walk through it, and he was a man who believed in keeping his word.

"I look forward very much to this aspect of old age — to lost scenes that will be restored to me in all their original freshness, and the clearing up of God knows what mistakes and uncertainties. The things I suddenly remember now, at fifty-nine, are not from this far down; that is, I remember that I have remembered them before, at intervals, and then forgotten them. And will again. The memory itself is not always very interesting, but if I stop and gather in all the strands that are attached to it, it is worth examining. Yesterday afternoon I had to transact by telephone some business of a highly detailed sort that called for accuracy and judgment at every moment, and the call went on for two hours and fifteen minutes. I had not slept well the night before and had had a taxing day, and from time to time during the last forty-five minutes of the call I would glance at the clock on the wall of my office and then at the thickness of the pile of sheets that remained to be dealt with. And several times a feeling of weakness, bordering on nausea, came over me and I wasn't sure that I was going to make it — to finish what had to be done, and done right then.

And suddenly I remembered being in a rowboat with my father and mother, on the Illinois River. I was perhaps a year or two older than I was that Sunday morning. Old enough, in any case, to perceive what I wouldn't have perceived at three. They had gone fishing, downstream from the resort we were staying in, and had taken me with them. We were at a place where the river widened out to become a lake, and one of those sudden Illinois thunderstorms had blown up, out of the heat and heaviness of the August afternoon. The sky was black, and there were whitecaps. And my father was rowing steadily toward the hotel landing, out of sight, around a bend in the river. I liked storms, and was not afraid of thunder and lightning. I was enjoying the wind and the peculiar light and all that excitement in the sky, until my father said, 'Bill, get down in the bottom of the boat.' In his voice I heard that he was afraid — a thing that I didn't know could happen! I did as he told me, and then looked at my mother for enlightenment. You know I trust your father absolutely but we're in trouble, is what I read in her face, and it isn't his fault, or anybody's, but we shouldn't be out here on the river, in a storm like this, in a rowboat. Stay as still as you can . . . Though I weighed no more than a feather, they were both heavy people, and my mother especially, and the stern of the rowboat sat low in the water. I can hear the creaking of the oarlocks, across half a century. My father is doing the best he can, but if the storm breaks while we are still out on this boat, what will become of us?

"I suppose we were there a week. During that time I was particularly interested in a showboat that was tied up at the dock, though we didn't get taken to any performance on it. We did make a night trip down the river in a paddlewheeled steamer. There was no theatrical company at the time, but the steamer took passengers up and down the river at night, and I remember looking at the garish, empty auditorium, and the lights strung up and down the decks. All this I am unsure about. But there is some memory that is trying to surface. I think a year later, perhaps even to the day, this steamer caught on fire and sank, with a considerable loss of life. Or have I mixed it with the sinking of the *Eastland,* in Chicago, at the same time. That tragedy occurred while the steamer was about at the dock, or just leaving it. The entire passenger list, on a heavily booked excursion, stood on one side of the steamer, waving goodbye to those on shore, and over it went. The decks were screened and they were all trapped, and sank with the steamer. One of those dreadful catastrophes that Chicago used to specialize in.

"What I remember is the feeling of destiny. The ship did not catch on fire when we were on it, but it could have; we had been close to a disaster, and something saved us."

When Maxwell and my father were seventy-five, my father mentioned in a letter the difficulties an elderly woman whom both of them knew, Katie May, was having because of her advanced age.

"Poor Katie," Maxwell wrote back. "Milton Greenstein," the lawyer for *The New Yorker,* "said about Hawley Truax, who was the treasurer of *The New Yorker* and lived to be ninety-six, that he had missed his chance to die. Shortly afterward, Hawley did in fact escape from this world and have a very nice Memorial Service at which the Minister read in a less droning voice than usual passages from the Bible and from Hawley's poetry. He was a Francophile and at the end of the service, as people stood up to go, the organist played the 'Marseillaise.' It was thrilling. Even though I admire my father-in-law and two or three other acquaintances who have lived on into their nineties, I hope to God I don't have to emulate them."

Having the floor rise up to meet you when you thought you had your balance is what he was afraid of. And the mind continuing its existence in a body it has outlived. When he was somewhere in the middle of his eighties, he said to me, "The nineties loom up before me with a kind of horror." It didn't turn out that way, though. When he was ninety I asked him what it was like. "I turned into an old man in a series of perceptions," he said. "You look into the mirror and see who you've been shaving. A terribly fortunate old man, active, not in a wheelchair and not using a cane."

About a year earlier, to the poet Edward Hirsch, in an

interview published in the magazine *DoubleTake,* he said something similar; rather, he wrote on his typewriter: "I am no longer surprised at being as old as I am because I went through two or three preliminary shocks that prepared me for it. They all occurred in front of the bathroom mirror while I was shaving. The first was, 'What am I doing attached to that old man?' The second, a few days later, was, 'But I don't want to leave the party.' There were others, but I have forgotten them. Now when I shave I am shaving the face I expect to shave. But somewhere, having a considerable influence on my feelings and behavior, the child survives, who expects (rather than intends) to live forever. The man says, not a good idea. But they don't argue about it."

As he got close to ninety, time began to behave like an accordion, he said; that is, it expanded and collapsed. Events that had been far apart no longer seemed separated by much distance at all. "I don't think of having children across a great gulf," he said, "but it's actually been forty years." What he had looked forward to when he was younger — the completion of scenes that had returned before only in fragments — actually occurred. In addition, his memory began to provide him with scenes of a kind that it hadn't before.

"These days, it's more that I'm rowing around on an ocean of experience," he said, "and the ocean is memory. Sometimes I lie awake at night thinking about the past, and it's as if I've put a record on the record player, and there's no way to stop it. It's a form of reliving, and I can't stop reliving it.

"In old age experience is prismatic. It's as if you're holding your life in your hands, turning it this way and that, and what you see are sides of a prism. It's half recollection and half a visual re-enactment of moments from the past, whereas when you're younger, you're simply living the experience. Quite recently, I have begun having flashes of memory so vivid that I see my mother sitting at the dining room table when I was four or five. She doesn't speak, and I can't touch her, but she's there. And the table is there, and the food is there. It's a little like she was in a store window, or as if it were a photograph capable of moving. In old age, not much is involved, really, in the life of the memory except understanding. You've taken the major actions and are going to have to stand by them."

He was sixty-eight when we began working together. As a young man he had spent a lot of time in the sun, and he had begun to need small surgeries to remove skin cancers from his face. One of them cost him a portion of his lower lip and another one part of his nose. Over the years more and more of his nose disappeared. My mind simply accommodated the changes, and I was surprised when I saw photographs of him in the scrapbooks my father had assembled, when he was younger and looked different.

I retain images of him from several periods that are like templates: the man who came and went from my parents' house, who was heavier and whose face was rounder and who still had some hair on the top of his head. The way he looked when we began working together, when his face wasn't round any longer but not gaunt, either. And his face near the end of his life, when his features had fallen into their final forms and were so spare and elemental, as if nothing was left of how he looked except what conveyed character and feeling.

When I see images of him made during the last years of his life, especially tapes of his being interviewed on television or ones made at readings — that is, pictures in which I can see his expression change, and hear his voice, which had become raspy and quiet, and observe the pauses for thought before he spoke, how sharp his features had grown, and how his wrist hardly filled his shirt cuff any longer, I realize what an old man he had become, but I didn't have that impression when he was alive.

I suppose he was a ruin of the handsome man he had been, but the light in his eyes was always lively. His observations, his judgment, his appraisals of writing or a person's character seemed no less acute than they ever had been. He never behaved in a way that made me feel his vitality had diminished, but he never would have mentioned it. Every now and then he spoke of how much discomfort Mrs. Maxwell was enduring and how it struck him as unjust.

I was attentive to some other part of him, his nature, I guess. His essential self, is what I would like to think, but of course part of my absorption must have been a refusal to face facts: he was advancing into deep old age. I think it is strange that I never took account of his aging. He looked to me at eighty and even at ninety as I had always thought of him. People would tell me that they had seen him recently and were concerned at how frail he had grown. And I would think, Really? And that the explanation for my not having noted the change must be that I was with him so often, I had no image in mind from the last time I saw him that differed materially from how he looked now. Or that I spent so much time looking into his eyes that I failed to observe him objectively.

I realize now that something unbearable was taking place: my closest friend was declining, and I refused to accept it. I don't mean that I resolved not to; I mean that the disaster approaching so unsettled me that my psyche could respond only by declining to acknowledge its imminence or even that it was happening. It was doing what it could to protect me from the distress of confronting what I couldn't seem to face. I don't know how else to explain it.

About a year before he died, he needed something from the house in the country, and we drove out one warm night and had dinner and stayed up until eleven, sitting in chairs on the porch and looking at the stars and talking, like people on the deck of a ship. He said that he was staying up later as he got older and sleeping later, and because he always enjoyed sleeping, I mistook this to be an indulgence in a pleasure.

I observed all the stages of his decline and failed to register any of them for what they were. We went walking one day along the river in the spring before he died, and he leaned into me suddenly, and said, "That seems to happen to me now. I lose my balance when I don't expect it. I don't think it's serious." Another day I met him, walking with a nurse, and saw that he needed to depend on her arm and that the slightest incline in the sidewalk caused him to stop and gather his breath.

He didn't look to me like someone who might die. I had seen my father die, the retreat into himself, the erosion of his personality, from mild strokes, I suppose; and though I could see that Maxwell was in worse and worse shape, he seemed in his nature as he ever had been. I thought that before anyone could die, the mind and the body had to separate, and that as long as he was in possession of himself, he remained some distance from the cemetery. Didn't there have to be a loss of consciousness, a crisis, or a wearing down, a gradual coming to a stop?

His daughters understood how fragile his hold on life was. They'd never thought that he would be with them forever, or even for much longer.

How odd of me not to have taken in that it would end. Maxwell never seemed ill to me. And when he was, I assumed he would recover.

*

In the last few months of his life Maxwell began using a magnifying glass to read, and not long after that he became unable to make out the words even with it. He had hoped to read as many of the books he loved as he could. He once said that the only thing that really bothered him about being dead was that there was no Tolstoy. When his eyes gave out, he was reading *War and Peace.* For weeks the writer Annabel Davis-Goff came every afternoon around four and read it to him and Mrs. Maxwell when she was well enough to join them. One morning when I arrived for a visit, I saw a book open on the coffee table and a magnifying glass beside it. Maxwell felt insufficiently informed about Napoleon's campaigns in Russia and had found a reference to a battle Tolstoy described. He had tried to read it with the magnifying glass and was waiting for me so that we could finish it.

I was uncertain about what to expect as the end of Maxwell's life approached. I wasn't a member of the family, I wasn't sure what role I had among them. Moreover, he might die suddenly, and there would be only a phone call. Or he might be sufficiently overtaken by illness or a stroke that he was no longer who I had known him to be. In his story "My Father's Friends," he wrote: "I must have been thirteen or fourteen when I heard that Aunt Beth had cancer and was in the hospital. I felt I ought to go see her. I thought my mother would want me to. My Aunt Annette was in Florida and there was no one to enlighten me about what to expect. I went from room to room of the hospital, reading the cards on the doors and peering past the white cloth screens, and on the second floor, in the corridor, I ran into her. She was wearing a hospital gown and her hair was in two braids down her back. Her color was ashen. She saw me, but it was as if she were looking at somebody she had never seen before. Since then, I have watched beloved animals dying. The withdrawal, into some part of themselves that only they know about. It is, I think, not uncommon to any kind of living creature. A doctor passed, in a white coat, and she turned and called after him urgently. I skittered down the stairs and got on my bicycle and rode away from the hospital feeling that I had made a mistake. I had and I hadn't. She was in no condition to receive visitors. But I had acquired an important item of knowledge — dying is something people have to live through, and while they are doing it, unless you are much closer to them than I was to her, you have little or no claim on them."

My father died in a matter of days. He had lost most of his memory and his ability to reason; it was as if the person he had been — the bluff, commanding, resilient, and forceful man — had deliquesced, or worn thin like a piece of fabric. My mother kept him home for as long as she could, but he was subject to manias — he took all the money out of his savings account one afternoon and tried to spend it at a store called the Christmas Tree Shop — and he was still strong enough to make opposing him difficult if he got it into his mind to do something my mother didn't want him to. She found a nursing home not far from their house. My brother Kirk, who is named for my father, delivered him there. My father appeared to know where he was going and that he wouldn't be home again. The night before, my brother sat beside him, and my father asked him to sing the ABCs with him. I think he was scared but couldn't find the words to say so. Instead he tried to soothe himself by enacting an experience of childhood. I am only guessing, of course.

In the nursing home he sat in a wheelchair, and each day his chin dropped lower on his chest. From his workshop I brought his watercolor paints and some brushes, and I filled a glass with water from the sink in his room and put some paper in front of him. He wet the brushes and stirred them in the cups of paint, then began to move the brush across the paper. His hand shook. He tried one color then another. As they bled together, he dropped the brush onto the paper. I am fairly sure that the words he managed to get out were "What's the use?" It was, in any case, the last time I heard him speak.

A few days later he lay down for a nap and didn't wake up. My mother seemed to feel that putting him in the home had brought about his dying, but there was nothing else she could have done.

"You've got him safely home at last," Maxwell wrote her. "It must have taken all the strength you had (and more) but you've done it.

"There was nobody like him in my life. There couldn't be."

When the summer arrived, my wife and my son and I moved for six weeks to Washington, D.C., so that my son could attend a camp that specializes in certain difficulties he endures. The plans had been made during the winter and couldn't be put aside; Maxwell insisted that we go. All spring it was on my mind that he might die while we were there.

What kept the Maxwells' household afloat was that Kate moved into her old bedroom, and, with the help of her sister, Brookie, and several of the Maxwells' friends, oversaw the nurses who came and went at all hours and the dispensing of medications and the exchanges with doctors and the meals and the shopping for food and all the other tasks the Maxwells could no longer manage. Observing Kate talking on the phone to her mother's doctor while holding her cell phone in her other hand, in case her father's doctor should call, I was put in mind of the turtle that some tribe believes bears the world on its back.

By the summer, Maxwell was still occupying the room he had shared with his wife; she had moved to a hospital bed in the room where she used to paint. Each afternoon he sat in a wheelchair by the side of her bed, and they talked and held hands.

Two people can never live beside each other in perfect intimacy, Maxwell once told me. One of the things she had concealed from him was that her illness was fatal. Or it may be that he knew but refused to acknowledge it. Almost two years earlier, she had been scheduled for an operation, and a screening of her blood found cancer cells. When the first course of chemotherapy didn't get rid of them, she had a second round, then a third — a year and a half altogether — then decided to stop, since it hadn't worked. Maxwell was under the impression that quitting would allow her body to heal itself, without interference from the chemicals. She grew thinner and more frail.

The Maxwells never talked about their difficulties; they were exceptionally discreet. I called every day and spoke to Maxwell, or to one of his daughters or his nurse if he wasn't able to come to the phone, and one evening in the middle of July, Kate said that several of her mother's relatives had paid a visit that afternoon and everyone in the household had gathered in her bedroom and that perhaps her mother's end was close at hand. I asked my wife whether it would be all right for me to fly the next morning to New York for the day.

When I arrived, there were a number of people in the apartment — the nurses, two or three of Mrs. Maxwell's friends, the Maxwells' daughters, and a young woman from Oregon who was the daughter of one of Mrs. Maxwell's childhood friends. For a few minutes I sat in the living room; then Kate came in and said, "Father would like to see you." The formality struck me as being like something from a Russian novel. Maxwell was sitting up in his bed, propped against the pillows. The state of his vision was such that he could make out no more of a person's identity than his profile. I stood in the doorway and he said, "Could it be?" As I think of the moment now, I recall only the happiness I felt at laying eyes on him. He held out his hand and I took it and held on to it. I sat beside him and told him how happy I was to see him and how much I had missed him. Kate appeared in the doorway now and then to see if he was tired. "I trust you to know that," she said. One of Maxwell's friends, the poet Michael Collier, came by, having taken the train up from Maryland for the day. After a while, I left them alone, because I assumed, since I planned to stay for the rest of the day, that I would have other chances to see him, and Collier might not.

Edward Hirsch also arrived. Maxwell was taken in to see his wife. I sat by the record player in the living room, listening to Ella Fitzgerald sing "Don't Fence Me In" and writing down the words; Brookie had had the idea that everyone could sing it to her mother. When I was finished, all of us went into her room. She was in the hospital bed. She wore a Chinese bed jacket made of silk, with a high collar, and there was a shawl across her chest. Her hair was short and boyish, and as thin as her face had become, it was still beautiful, and her eyes were still radiant. Some of her paintings were turned to the wall and others hung where she could see them. When she saw me, she remembered that years ago I had a pair of dogs that would howl if I did, as if they were singing. I remembered that my father once told Maxwell, "If anything ever happens to you, don't worry. I'll marry Emmy." We stood around her bed. She mentioned that my son was the child who tried to get into the candlebox house, which no one quite understood except Maxwell and her daughters. Later, Brookie showed me in the living room the small porcelain house, a candle holder, with windows that a child might think he could climb through.

Mrs. Maxwell said, "I think we should open a bottle of champagne." Standing in a half circle around her, holding our glasses, we sang "Don't Fence Me In." Maxwell held her hand and she closed her eyes and softly sang some of the words. She opened her eyes when we came to the end and said, "Lovely." Then she closed her eyes once more. "I'm going to slip away now for a while," she said. She wanted to listen to "Death and the Maiden," by Schubert, and Kate went to look for the tape of it.

Each of us leaned over the bed to kiss her as we left. "This is the most difficult thing I've ever had to do," she told Edward Hirsch. "Rilke said that each of us must die his own individual death, and now I have to die mine." Such courage.

*

That evening at dinner I sat between Maxwell, in his wheelchair, and Shirley Hazzard, who came often to the apartment and sat in the living room if the Maxwells weren't well enough to see her. She and the Maxwells had been friends for nearly forty years, since she had begun selling stories to *The New Yorker*. The table was crowded. None of us wanted to be anywhere else. Hazzard had been married for years to Francis Steegmuller, who had been a young reporter at *The New Yorker* when Maxwell started working there. Steegmuller was tall and lanky and somehow looked more French than American. He was immensely erudite and funny and gracious and incorruptible, a true friend. His translation of *Madame Bovary* is regarded as definitive. When he finished it, he told Maxwell, "Only one man stands between me and the writing of *Madame Bovary*." The Steegmullers lived a great deal of the time in Italy, and for a period they had a Rolls-Royce and employed a driver. Steegmuller had bought the car with royalties from his translation into French of "The Owl and the Pussycat," which had taken him an afternoon. Hazzard said that for a time it was necessary for them to take the car out of the country every six months, or the government would claim it and they would have to buy it back. They found themselves taken up during this period, somewhat mysteriously, by a rich crowd. One night at dinner, one of the women said to Steegmuller, "I wonder if you would take a painting for me across the border to Switzerland wrapped up in the trunk." Steegmuller said, "I couldn't do that." The woman, a little flustered, said, "Of course, I wouldn't ask you to do anything illegal," and he said, "I thought you were."

Maxwell didn't say much, but he was completely engaged by the conversation. After he had gone to bed and the dishes were collected, I called my wife, Sara, and asked if she minded if I stayed another day. She was very close to the Maxwells, and I knew it pained her not to see them. Maxwell had once said to me, "I don't know when Sara became one of my children, but she is."

I rode back to my apartment on the bus with Annabel Davis-Goff. She said, "Did you have a leave-taking with Bill?" I said I hadn't and asked if she had. "Yes, he called me in and we sat and talked, and I felt that it was a leave-taking." Why I hadn't, I didn't know.

When I arrived the next morning, Maxwell wasn't yet awake. During the night Mrs. Maxwell had lapsed into unconsciousness. She lay, her head to one side, breathing very slowly. There was music playing. A friend sat by one side of the bed, and a nurse sat by the other.

After he had had breakfast Maxwell said, "You must go home. Sara and Sam need you." The young woman from Oregon, Elizabeth Raglione, was leaving that afternoon, and I thought I would attach myself to her, share a taxi to the airport, and somehow, putting one foot in front of the other, I would arrive where I was supposed to be.

When I went in to say I would be leaving, Maxwell

was lying in bed, not strong enough to sit up. I lay down beside him. He said, "There's something you should know." He could draw enough breath for only one sentence at a time. "If I can get out of this world by not eating, I'm going to."

"Could you leave if you wanted to?"

"Oh, yes. I could close my eyes and leave now, if I wanted to," he said, "but I can't." I understood him to mean that he wouldn't so long as Mrs. Maxwell was alive.

"It must pain you terribly to see Emmy this way."

"I held her hand," he said, and he shrugged. "There was a pressure. She seemed to know I was there."

I helped him sit up then and take some pills. He asked for the biggest ones first. He had always told me that in writing I should begin with the hardest thing, so that once it was done I would have momentum.

When it was time for Elizabeth and me to leave, Maxwell was in the living room with visitors. I would be passing through the city in two weeks, so I said, "I'll see you week after next." And because he had guests and because I had spent my time with him so intimately, I simply waved, and we left.

On the phone the next morning he said, "Kate came in at Christ knows what hour it was and told me, 'She's gone.' And I went in, and she was lying on her side, and I touched her hand, and all I could remember was how cold my mother's hand had been as a corpse, and

Emmy's wasn't cold at all. The warmth stayed in for, I don't know, the two hours that I sat there. And I found myself telling her stories about my remote past, which Brookie loves to hear, and I talked until I was exhausted."

He paused. "When I think of her with the music and the champagne, and her with her eyes closed, singing, and all the voices," he said, "it's all so beautiful."

On the following day, people came to the apartment to pay their respects. Maxwell kept to his bedroom. The visitors stayed in the living room. The ones he felt able to see his nurse brought to him and allowed them to stay only two minutes.

The next day on the phone he said, "Yesterday was the strangest day. So many things went on, comic and peculiar, mostly comic. I had the odd sensation of being both the mourner and the corpse. People kept coming all day long. A writer I had edited sat down and wanted to talk about *The New Yorker*. Everyone wanted to resume the old relationships; it was so dear. I heard Ellis explaining the whole thing in the other room. He said, 'Grandma died, so we can't see her, but she can see us. And she can't read me books anymore, but she's in heaven.'"

I said how difficult I had found it to leave the apartment and that I had been able to only by imagining myself responsible for getting Elizabeth to the airport. After she got out of the car, I had wanted to tell the driver to take me back to the city.

"I wouldn't have been surprised if you had showed up," he said.

He sounded tired. His breath came slowly.

"I should let you go," I said.

"All right," he said. "I don't think we'll stop talking just because I'm dead."

A leave-taking is what it sounded like. I asked my wife whether she could manage if I went back to New York, and within two hours I had taken a taxi to the airport, boarded the shuttle, got a taxi to East Eighty-sixth Street, and was walking through the door of the Maxwells' apartment. No one was in the living room, so I went to Maxwell's bedroom. I was so happy to see him, so relieved, really, that I said, "It's like a love affair; I can't stay away." He held his arms toward me and we embraced, and I sat on the bed beside him.

He was extremely thin and frail, and I knew he must be dying, but all I felt was the happiness of being with him. I still don't quite understand this. How I could manage to feel joy in the face of such dire circumstances. It was a form of exultation, the likes of which I have seen since in people given news they cannot absorb. Plainly, no one else seemed in the grip of such a feeling. Was it one part of my mind subduing another? Or the result of my having lived for years with an awareness that time was growing short? His eyes had all the warmth they ever had; he remained the kind, benevolent presence he always had been to me.

The last few weeks I felt no restraint to expressing my affection for him. What would have been the point. I sat on his bed, sometimes with my arms around him, sometimes holding his hand, and his daughters and other friends did the same. The intimacy was offhand and un-self-conscious. It was as if we had found a new plane to occupy. One day when I arrived Maxwell was sitting with his legs over the side of his bed, and he looked up and said, "I'm a smelly mess; I'm so ashamed," but I hadn't noticed anything discomfiting, and I didn't after he said it. I loved him and wanted to do for him anything that I could.

When I held him I was conscious of the hard bones, so frail, and the necessity for being gentle. If I was present when he needed to get to his feet, I put my hands and arms where the nurse, standing on his other side, told me to and waited until she said, "Ready? . . . OK . . . *Up*." The responsibility felt enormous.

What I also knew was that nothing separated us any longer, no social obstacle, anyway. There was nothing more to happen between us. We were as if riding on a river together, in a small boat, and felt calm. All the afternoons sitting beside each other at the desk in his study in the country, or at a card table set up on a lawn looking toward a pond, all the meals and the wine and the champagne, all the talk and affection, all the dependence on his judgment, the attending to his voice, had led to this room and sitting beside him, holding his hand, and feeling love, which was itself worn like a garment over a sadness that was part loneliness and part despair and anger at being deprived of the one man I loved.

That day Maxwell came to the table for lunch, and I sat next to him. He ate four oysters on the half shell. "I don't understand what's happening to me," he said. "I was a private person. I never had a best seller."

"What do you mean?"

"All the people," he said. "It's as if they were gathering under my window to sing to me."

"You never knew what you meant to everyone?"

"No."

"I've never known anyone as widely loved as you and Emmy."

"Other people's work gave me so much pleasure," he said. Then he shrugged and said, "I'm a very spiritual man, but my religion is literature. It wouldn't do for the priest to take himself too seriously."

The sun was shining and it was mild outdoors, and I suggested to his nurse that I take Maxwell for a walk in his wheelchair along the promenade by the river, something he had done for years, first to walk the family dog, and then on his own for pleasure. She said that his body gave him so much pain that he could no longer tolerate the bumps he might receive. He had canceled a visit to his doctor that morning because he couldn't bear the idea of getting into a taxi and being bounced around.

No one had expected him to do anything but depart

once Mrs. Maxwell died, as if he had set a clock to her. When Mrs. Maxwell had first been diagnosed with her illness, Brookie said to me, "Father won't last six months without her." Mrs. Maxwell was from a family in which everyone had lived to an advanced age, and it was always assumed that she would outlast him. Maxwell had years before told me that after he died he thought she might move back to Oregon, but I don't know if she would have. She loved New York City and her friends there and her daughters and her grandson. I had hoped she wouldn't, because I had imagined seeing her often.

On the fourth day after Mrs. Maxwell died, Edward Hirsch and I sat on Maxwell's bed, and he told us that during the night he had resolved to live as long as he could. "I need to be here for my children," he said, "and for my grandson." He began eating again. He had his nurse make appointments with the doctors he needed to see, and he resumed taking his medications. Watching Mrs. Maxwell die had been like witnessing a remorseless process of nature unfold. Maxwell seemed simply to be growing more and more feeble and tired.

He began talking about the lightness of being. He said that he felt like one of those insects that shed their bodies for another one.

That morning I ran hot water over a washcloth, held it to his cheeks, then lathered a brush and spread shaving soap on them. He sat with his eyes closed. His breath came so slowly, he hardly seemed to be breathing at all. As gently as I tried to move the razor across his cheek, it still caught here and there, and he winced. He said nothing. It was as if he were far away, in another territory.

From his bedroom Maxwell sent a note to Kate saying that his friends should take from the apartment anything of his that they cared to, and she asked me if I wanted anything in particular. I said that I would happily take whatever no one else wanted, which was the truth, but only partly. It was difficult to balance the desire to have certain of his possessions for the comfort they would bring, and the feeling of being too avidly interested. So I dissembled. Kate said she would tell her father that I had offered to take what remained, and later she came to me and said, "He told me, 'Tell Alec he shouldn't go around with so much baggage.'"

All his life Maxwell had been fond of sleeping and dreaming. He once wrote that he imagined death as being something like lying down to an afternoon nap that has no end. Sitting on his bed, I asked him if he still had dreams, and he said, "Oh, yes. The taxis that are full when I need one. Or the taxi with its light on that goes beyond me and picks up another man. I've been having this dream for thirty or forty years. Sometimes it's trains, too. It's time for the train to leave and I'm still packing. I've never had a moment when I've thought, 'Oh, that's it; now I understand what this means. They're very real taxis, and they're not stopping for me.'"

He paused. Then he said, "It's the strangest thing. When I'm awake I keep asking myself, 'Where's Emmy?' It's not any particular kind of grieving; it's just the mind trying to find her."

I remembered that he had once said to me, after my father had died, "I was reading this afternoon and suddenly into my mind came the thought, *Kirk is no more.*"

Two days before Maxwell died, he sat on a chair in his bedroom, wearing his pajamas and wrapped in a blanket like a refugee or an Indian chief. His lawyer sat facing him, and with Kate and a few other friends they discussed Maxwell's will. When the lawyer asked if there were instructions for his literary executor, Maxwell said, "No movies, no plays, no adaptations of any kind."

I said, "What if someone wants to arrange a reading?"

"No dramatic readings," he said. "Of anything."

"At all?"

"Nothing."

Maxwell had never allowed anyone to turn his novels or stories into movies or to present a version of them on the stage. He was not indifferent to money, but there were things that he wouldn't do for it. He had worked hard to see that the writing he published reflected his intentions, and he did not care to know anyone else's interpretation of them, no matter what the financial benefit might have been or who was interested. He especially didn't want an actor's face to come to mind when someone spoke of one of his characters.

When he was just married, and before his daughters were born, when he was, that is, in his early forties, Maxwell wrote to his father: "To be even a first-rate writer, let alone a great one, something is asked of you that is asked only of artists — whether they be painters or musicians or what have you, and that involves the imagination and also strangely a moral problem. Do you remember the story in the Bible of how Jacob wrestled all night with the angel and would not let him go until the angel blessed him? In a way that's every artist's struggle — how to win the angel's blessing. It's symbolical, of course, and yet it has literal truth and meaning. The angel is the artist's own talent, the extent of which he has very little idea of . . .

"The older I get, the more reason I find to hope that my talent is substantial, and that I may, before I die, accomplish something of permanent value, but it requires something like self-dedication. It means saying no to Hollywood and the general temptations of easy money, which have been for some time at my elbow. It means also that everything I do has to have the very best and whole of me in it. And that no other consideration shall take precedence over the problem of holding a mirror up to life. At this point morality enters, because of course there is not merely one kind but two. The first says you are not only an artist but a man as well, with a responsibility toward the family you were born into, toward your wife, your father, toward Grace [his stepmother], who was good to you, toward *The New Yorker,* toward — the line forms on the right and extends over the horizon and out of sight. In the past I have often knocked myself out, worrying lest something I wrote would cause embarrassment, make trouble, hurt somebody's feelings, make life difficult for somebody I loved. I have tried to rearrange the truth of my own version in such a way that it would be intact and still not inflict pain on anyone who saw himself in the mirror. As you know, it hasn't been too successful a compromise. There are times when you can rearrange the truth and times when it can't be rearranged, and so you have to lop off a little here and a little there, which would be fine if you could come back from the grave and restore the missing parts. But every novel and every story that appears has to stand, at the moment of its appearance, as final, as the best I have in me to do, with only a limited lifetime to do it in. At this point the second morality enters and says either you serve *me,* artistic morality, wholeheartedly and honestly, or you are a fake, Bill Maxwell. You are only partially an artist and a partial accomplishment is the most you'll ever have.

"Fortunately, Emmy is with me, willing to make sacrifices, any sacrifice I ask of her, and some of them are painful. I feel you are with me too, and always have been . . ."

Having stated his feelings was perhaps sufficient for his purposes. Or he thought his father might not understand. In any case, he put the letter into a folder instead of sending it.

The next morning when I arrived at Maxwell's apartment, he was sitting with his feet over the side of the bed, and his nurse was beside him. He had his head down, as if he were making a small graceful bow, and when he finally raised it he said, "I'm in the depths of something . . . Sleep, I guess." He drank some orange juice, and then I held his coffee cup for him and he sipped from it occasionally. He said that my brother Leland, who lives in Chicago, and is an accomplished pianist, had called him the evening before and put the phone down by his piano and played for him. As a boy, Leland had taken lessons from Jean Dansereau, who had been forced to give up his concert career because he was susceptible to stage fright. Dansereau lived across the road from the Maxwells, in a house that had been a cider mill in the nineteenth century. When the weather allowed it, he opened the windows of the house and sat down to play, and if the wind was blowing in the right direction Maxwell could hear him. Chopin, mostly, and Debussy, and Liszt and Schumann and Schubert. In middle age, Maxwell had studied with Dansereau, and given up only when he realized that he was playing the piano when he might have been writing. Dansereau had a forceful personality, and he was a demanding teacher. He had held a position in my brother's life something like the one Maxwell later occupied for me.

"Leland's playing was so striking," Maxwell said. "He played some Chopin and some Schumann, which I like more. It was very complicated playing, full of feeling and dexterity, but you could hear Jean in it. It was as if he had cast a spell over him and wouldn't let go."

Someone once remarked that all writers are children and need to be told once a day that what they have written and published is good. All a writer can know with certainty is whether the writing is the best he or she is capable of. I was plagued for years by the anxiety that Maxwell might not be proud of my work and the role he had played in bringing so much of it about. The subject had never come up between us, and I knew I couldn't ask him. He would tell me only as much of the truth as he thought I could bear, and that might involve his saying yes when he didn't mean it. I had accepted the notion that I would never know for sure what he felt.

I wonder now why I treated myself so severely. He knew how to deflect someone gently; I had seen him do it on more than one occasion. If he had reservations about helping me, he would have found some means of disengaging himself. There is no more I can teach you, he might have said. Or, What's most important now is that you form your own impression of your work.

The day before he died we were sitting on his bed and he said, "There is another thing I need to tell you. I received a letter from a group that gives an award, asking me to suggest someone, and I suggested you."

There were many writers he might have put forth, of course, and if he had named someone other than me I couldn't have felt that I had been shortchanged.

"It would be great to get it," I said.

He nodded.

Maxwell never gave another writer a quote to be used in promoting his or her work. He felt that his being an editor made it unfair for him to endorse one writer and not another, or one book and not another, and that if he gave a statement to one writer, he'd be obliged to give one to all of them. I had once asked him to say something about one of my books, and he said that he couldn't, because of the writers who might justifiably be aggrieved if they saw it. I felt that his willingness to have his name connected to mine in the minds of the people who had asked for his nomination was as strong an endorsement as it would have been possible to receive from him. He wouldn't have wished, I knew, to have his name attached, even in private, to someone whose work he deplored.

"What pleases me the most," I said, "is that I always wondered if you were proud of me."

It is odd how things sometimes arrive after one has given up hoping they would. When I need cheering, or at moments when my courage is failing, I repeat what he said; rather, I close my eyes and hear him say it.

"Oh, yes, I'm proud of you."

I feel it almost as an embrace.

The secret of the afterlife is nothing, Maxwell once

wrote, compared to all the secrets the dead take with them when they go.

Now and then I reflect that I might have spent the rest of my life without knowing. An impoverishment is what it would have amounted to.

That afternoon Maxwell sat in his pajamas in a chair in the living room, with a blanket around his shoulders. He had been in the habit of getting dressed for a few hours each afternoon to see people, and this was the first day that he hadn't. Edward Hirsch knelt on one side of his chair and I knelt on the other, and we opened his mail and read it to him. There were more letters about Mrs. Maxwell than he could possibly answer. One of us would read a letter, and he would close his eyes for so long that I wondered if he had drifted off, but then he would frame a sentence and I would write it down. He had not the energy for more than a few words at a time.

To a young man who wrote that he would never forget him, Maxwell answered, "Nor I you." To his agent, who had been so attentive, "How do you thank someone for saving your life?" To one of Brookie's friends, who wrote two pages about how much he had enjoyed being with the Maxwells and how much he had loved Mrs. Maxwell, "The pleasure was all ours." To a young writer who in Maxwell's opinion spent too much time showing his book to agents and not editors, he said, "Get on with it." The response provoked by someone the Maxwells had known for years but whose character Maxwell viewed as slight was "What I want to say is that there is more to life than social climbing, but I can't." He put the letter aside until he could think of something else. I asked if I should sign the letters *Love,* and he said, "Why stint anyone at this point?" When a letter was from someone he didn't care to answer — a writer who had given him a condescending review but still pursued his friendship, a photographer trying to interest him in using a picture of him and Mrs. Maxwell at a memorial — he simply shook his head.

His capacity for intimacy was such that I felt he was addressing these people as if they were in the room.

The next morning I found him sitting on his bed and drinking a glass of orange juice. I sat down beside him. The nurse handed me the glass and left. We sat for some time before he drew a deep breath and looked at me. "It's just that I'm made out of clouds," he said.

We talked about writing. I told him how much I liked making sentences.

"Stopping and starting," he said. The effort of drawing breath seemed to require his attention, and each phrase depleted him.

"To imitate the sounds of birds," he said . . .

"Or waves on the beach . . .

"To imitate anything."

I stood in the doorway of his room to say goodbye. He was lying on his side, turned away from me, with his knees drawn up. At the end of each long interval, his shoulders rose slightly and fell. I thought it better not to wake him.

Collected in a book of five of Maxwell's fables, which Mrs. Maxwell published privately for his eightieth birthday, is one about an elderly farmer who was benignly interested only in perfection. The chickens the farmer raised laid perfect eggs, because he studied what they needed — rest and good food, and room in the chicken house to wander around in. One fall he found a perfect maple leaf lying on the ground, which he varnished to his gatepost so that it never lost its colors or grew tattered and it gave him pleasure through the winter, and a perfect blue-jay feather he kept in a box. Then, because periods of rain or dryness altered the sound of the brook that ran through his pasture, he began to dam the brook and dig pools here and there to insure that the flow of water over the rocks and against the banks remained steady.

"After that he turned his attention to the sky," Maxwell wrote, "selecting and rejecting one sunrise, one sunset, after another, searching for the perfect moment between day and dusk and not knowing what he would do when he found it. Also the perfect star. The perfect blue patch of sky seen through pine branches. The odor of frost coming out of the ground. The smell of cows in a barn, feeding contentedly. The perfect spring day.

"With so many things to occupy his mind, he hardly noticed that his hair was turning white, that he stooped when he walked, and that he needed less and less sleep, as all old people do when they are nearing the end of their life. But one day, walking through a strange house, he saw himself in a mirror when he was not expecting to, and perceived by the great changes in his face that he did not have very much longer to live. So he began to reflect upon the perfect death. Most people would have said that it was to die in one's sleep. After considering this carefully, he rejected it. It was based on fear. He wanted to know when death happened. And he began to practice dying. But there are some things that can only be done by analogy, so he didn't cut himself badly or fall and break his hip, he merely practiced breathing in and out, and counting one two three four five six seven eight nine ten, one two three and so on, letting the air out of his lungs and waiting attentively for a kind of flip deep down in his chest, at which moment he stopped breathing out and began to breathe in. He became quite perfect at this, so that he could do it lying down or standing up or walking around and finally it just happened without his doing anything about it, or even having to count. And people thought he was growing deaf because he didn't hear what they said, but the truth was he had stopped being interested in anything they might have to say to him and instead was waiting for the day when he would come down with influenza and take to his bed, knowing he would never get up from it. And of course the day came, and so did the doctor, and in spite of the medicine he prescribed the old man's fever rose higher and higher, bringing images of the evening star or willow trees reflected in a still pond, and his breathing grew harsher and harsher, and in his delirium he counted soundlessly, one, two, three, four, five, until the moment came, as he knew it would, when he stepped out of this imperfect world into utter perfection and became one with the maple leaf, and the sound of the brook, and the blue-jay's feather."

I was under the impression that the next morning Maxwell sat up and had a little to eat and drank some coffee and then lay down and fell asleep and his heart stopped beating, but actually he never woke up. The woman who brought him his orange juice noticed that something about him was different.

On the phone, Kate told me, "He was talking last night about going South and how he wanted to go to the Kentucky farm where they fix horses and saddling up." Each summer in his mother's childhood, her parents had taken her to a farm in Kentucky that belonged to her grandparents.

I called my mother. That morning, she had had a letter from him. "Dear Carolyn," it read in the handwriting of whomever he had dictated it to. "Thank you for Alec. And weren't they nice times. Love, Bill."

As I walked to buy the newspapers the next morning to read what had been written about him, I saw three women on a corner talking, and in the moment before my mind focused I thought, They're talking about Bill. The notice of his death appeared on the front page of the New York *Times*.

A few days earlier, Maxwell had sent someone to the house in the country to collect from his desk the box that Mrs. Maxwell had painted for his ninetieth birthday. When his body was released to the flames, he wanted the box with him.

Nearly two months later, my wife and I were almost the last ones left on the lawn beside the cathedral. A child took the day's last ride on the back of the pony. I felt unable to come to terms with the idea that such a crowd would never be gathered again, not that collection of people, and not in that fashion, with the Maxwells the occasion, so much on everyone's mind and so vividly remembered. I left, because it was time for Sara and me to relieve our sitter, but in a frame of mind as if I had been stunned, or was obeying a summons, simply getting into the taxi and telling the driver our address, unable to reconcile myself the whole time.

After the memorial the pictures of the Maxwells that had been on display were brought back to the Maxwells' apartment. There was a small snapshot someone had taken from the doorway of Mrs. Maxwell's room not long before she died. Somehow I had overlooked it. Maxwell is sitting in a wheelchair beside her bed. The two of them are hardly more than skeletons. They are talking, or they are sitting quietly with each other; in any case, each is looking into the other's eyes. The picture suggests something of the invincibility of love. Fifty-five years of each other's company, night and day, and then the arrival at this end, where each is ravaged, neither of them able to walk to the other or even to embrace the other. The beautiful woman, so gifted, so irresistible, and the man, so sensitive, loving, and original, who had failed to be like other people; the child no one thought would have the strength to stay out of the cemetery; the boy who his relations thought wouldn't be sturdy enough for mature life; the young man his father worried wouldn't be able to support himself except by borrowing money; the two of them having endured, the formidable courage such an existence required. The light came through the windows beside them, and each attended the other closely, as they had all their lives together.

The beautiful tables and chairs that had come down through Mrs. Maxwell's family went to the country or to the apartments of their daughters or into storage. Mrs. Maxwell's paintings were put in crates. Maxwell's books were boxed. The china was wrapped. His clothes were given away. As the apartment came closer and closer to being emptied, I had the sensation that it was dying also. Its life had derived from the warmth they gave it. The rooms seemed to shrink to skin and bones and then to lose any sense of vitality at all. I didn't know that a place could lose its spirit, but it did. It had always been for me a refuge. When I sat on the couch with them, talking and drinking tea or champagne, the anxieties of the world felt remote. I felt as if nothing could lay a glove on me while I was with them. Now the place just seemed like a series of rooms that had no special character and needed plaster and paint.

Those last days were comforting. The embraces, the sitting quietly with Maxwell and saying nothing. Lying on the bed with my head close to his and talking on those occasions when he didn't have the strength to sit up. Shaving him. Holding his coffee until he was ready to accept it. Helping him stand when he needed to find his way to the bathroom or from his wheelchair into a chair in the living room so that he could talk to the people who had come to see him. The soft, glowing warmth of his eyes. His great dignity, so natural and unforced, so courageous, never faltering when his death was near. His being so present in his mind. His compassion. His sympathy. His great capacity for friendship.

What kind of life he saved me from I am not sure. Maxwell was privy to every decision of any consequence that I made during the last twenty-five years, and who I might have been in the absence of his influence I am the last person to say.

What happened between Maxwell and me allows me to know that my father was someone of greater breadth than who I took him to be. His failings were obvious —

his aptitude for harming others, his insensitivity. But he was also a great friend to this great man, and I am a mixture of them both. I would not have had the opportunity to be so if Maxwell had shaken my father's hand on the train platform and thought of how to disengage himself.

It is borne in on me that the calm and pleasure I felt in Maxwell's company, and the absence of any need to remark on it through periods of silence, was like the state of awareness that he and my father shared in the jeep on the way to the train station in the morning and home from it at night. Side by side like an old married couple. "Cold," one of them says. The other, staring straight ahead, only nods. The love that I felt for Maxwell is something my father felt also, and I am cheered by knowing that, despite all the patterns of my nature I inherited from him, all the attitudes and gestures I believe are his, some of which I have tried to cleanse from myself, all the disappointments he inflicted on me, I am his son in this way: we both embraced the same man, we were both soothed and enlarged by his company, and warmed by being with him, and wanted to do for him things that would make him happy.

I think of my father as someone who had very few moments of happiness. Sexual variety doesn't seem to me an acceptable replacement for love. If I imagine him as being my age, I see him as tormented and confused and uncertain in his judgments. In over his head, really. I know that he disliked the editor he worked for and felt that she went out of her way to torment him. He tried to have her fired and couldn't.

The excitement involved in having a clandestine sexual life might have been diverting for a while, but once that was eclipsed, you'd be left with the feeling of having piled up memories and experiences that offered little consolation and perhaps even haunted you. Maybe it is only that I am not built for such a life. Still, I know that in his early sixties, my father found himself involved in an affair that he was unable to break off. To extricate himself, he retired early, without telling anyone why, and he and my mother moved to their house on Cape Cod. They bought the art gallery. The woman my father had been trying to escape was someone my mother knew as the wife of a friend of my father's. She wrote my mother a letter. My father saw the envelope on my mother's desk and recognized the return address. The letter had already been opened.

I found out about all of this years later.

None of it is something I would care to live through.

My experience is that the impulses that guide us have a multiplicity of purposes, so that even while I wasn't entirely aware of my conflicted feelings for my father, I was being drawn to someone whose manner toward me would allow me eventually to resolve them.

I had been expecting to see Maxwell again. The life force in him seemed sufficiently intense that it wouldn't be easy to persuade it to quit. Perhaps this was also a form of denial, since no one else seemed to think it was true. I felt there was something in him determined to take part in life, even though he no longer left his apartment. When you talked to him, he asked what was going on in your life; he might say, "I lay awake last night worrying about how you're going to manage" this or that, is how the sentence would continue. Four days before Mrs. Maxwell died, the two of them went in wheelchairs to the Metropolitan Museum of Art to see a show of paintings by Chardin. He insisted to a friend that he see them also. The friend didn't go the day he said he would. Maxwell called him and told him not to hesitate. I want to talk to you about them, is what he added.

Nothing is more insistent on the unreality of someone's absence than the way he left things — his clothes in a closet, his keys on the hall table, his desk with the pencils needing to be sharpened, the eraser, the books by the side of the bed. The view out the window. You try to feel the person's presence as you look out at what he took in every morning. It's a form of impersonation. Some people are more sensitive to this than others, and I have never been a person who sees ghosts. I was willing to believe in the Ouija board. I asked Maxwell if he would come back for that, and he said no. Once he was gone, he intended to stay gone.

He wasn't interested in the kind of legacy that rests on other people's attention. He knew the value of his work and its place. He never cared especially for acclaim. At least he never sought it. "I collect readers one at a time," he once said. The day before he died, a friend and I were sitting with him and one of us made a joke about an award that Maxwell perhaps should have received, and he drew his breath and said, in a whispery voice, "Tell them . . . their fucking honors . . . mean nothing to me." I loved his defiance. Its passionate quality, the knowledge that the individual is sufficient if his work is, that no amount of social or commercial attention elevates a person's natural worth.

Maxwell believed that existence in any form is a privilege, and that people ought to have more courage. And that we were put on earth to be helpful to one another. And that nothing bad can happen, because it can't — a belief he based on his own good fortune, but that he knew had no rational basis and was indefensible. It was something he told people who were frightened, to give them hope, but what it amounted to, he knew, was superstition. When his daughters were little he sometimes took them to church, as a form of protective coloration, and he liked hearing the singing of the hymns, but his mind wandered when the Scriptures were read and verged into restlessness during the sermon.

One evening years ago in Yorktown, after we had finished working and were sitting in front of the fireplace, he asked me, "Are you religious?" Quite some time later, when I heard him ask another young person the same question, it occurred to me that he asked it of people when he suspected that they had been drawn to him as the result of a misimpression. Because it was apparent to anyone who met him that his nature was sensitive and sympathetic and receptive to shades of feeling, and because of the patience and objectivity and wisdom that typify his writing, people with a mystical cast of mind often thought that he held the same views that they did.

At twelve — not long after his mother died, that is — he joined the Presbyterian church. "Then we moved to Chicago," he told me, "and for the first time I went to a high school with a good library, and I read Mark Twain's *The Mysterious Stranger.* I had heard that it was a dangerous and heretical book, and I thought it wouldn't shake my faith, so as a test I read it, and it did shake my faith. It's an account of all the world's floods and fires and wars and catastrophes and what people do to each other, mass executions. To pretend that all these are the intentions of a benevolent God Mark Twain found hard to swallow. What sensible person can fail to be astonished in the face of creation? But people think that God cares about what happens to them. As a child I saw no evidence of any personal interest on God's part in our lives, and I still don't. Theologically speaking, it's not a sophisticated point of view, but it made sense to me."

Henry James wrote in a letter (to Grace Norton, on July 28, 1883): "I don't know *why* we live — the gift of life comes to us from I don't know what source or for what purpose; but I believe we can go on living for the reason that (always of course up to a certain point) life is the most valuable thing we know anything about, and it is therefore presumptively a great mistake to surrender it while there is any yet left in the cup. In other words consciousness is an illimitable power, and though at times it may seem to be all consciousness of misery, yet in the way it propagates itself from wave to wave, so that we never cease to feel, and though at moments we appear to, try to, pray to, there is something that holds one in one's place, makes it a standpoint in the universe which it is probably not good to forsake ... We all live together, and those of us who love and know, live so most. We help each other — even unconsciously, each in our own effort, we lighten the effort of others, we contribute to the sum of success, make it possible for others to live. Sorrow comes in great waves ... but it rolls over us, and though it may almost smother us it leaves us on the spot, and we know that if it is strong we are stronger, inasmuch as it passes and we remain. It wears us, uses us, but we wear it and use it in return; and it is blind, whereas we after a manner see."

As an elderly man, Maxwell sat at his typewriter and slowly copied out the letter. I know it was late in his life, because the characters resemble those on the typewriter he used for the last twenty years, and I know it was slowly because there are no mistakes, and his letters always included a few. I found the copy after he died, when I took down one of James's novels from its shelf by the fireplace in the living room of the house in the country.

*

I am sorry that I was not with Maxwell when he passed away. I am sorry I did not get to see him with his eyes closed, departed, free of all concerns, never again facing a bank statement, or an income tax form, or someone who wants something from you that you don't want to give them, or someone you resent or who intends you harm, someone you dislike, any kind of violence, any suffering. No pleasure anymore, but it's not my impression that his life was short on pleasure. "When I die, I hope people won't grieve for me," he once said. "I've had a very happy life."

I intended not to grieve. I resolved instead to feel only grateful for his friendship, for all the things he did for me, for his having taught me to be a writer, for providing me when I was young with a model of masculinity that was sensitive and appealing and courtly and had great dignity and was graceful. (If you wonder what kind of graceful, I can tell you that John Updike once described Maxwell as a figure resembling Fred Astaire.) Any reaction other than resignation seemed unrealistic. The world can't go on forever as it is; the future is never a continuation of the present. I felt thankful that he had lived as long as he had. A man who dies at, say, sixty-eight or seventy, or even seventy-five, is not generally thought to have died too early. Many men of Maxwell's generation died within a few years of having retired.

When someone dies it becomes more and more difficult to hold in mind an image of what he looked like. The harder one tries, the more difficult it becomes.

Perhaps this is protective, a vagueness intended to subdue our grief. I had the impression for days after Maxwell died that I hadn't paid close enough attention, that I should have made a record of everything he said at dinner parties and teas and over bottles of champagne, that I hadn't seen him often enough. I have read that there are stages of grief, and I suppose they are conventional and can't be avoided, like stages of an illness, but nonetheless I had hoped to escape them.

It turns out that such a resolution is not within my control. The deeper layers of memory are indifferent to time — it is why we can feel ourselves to be simultaneously seven or fifteen or twenty-five or the age we are — and they are also resistant to being dominated by simple intention. Everyone knows this, and I can't help wondering why I expected such rules not to apply in my case, except that most lessons in life are learned through experience, and I hadn't been exposed yet to this one.

In a state that is something like a reverie, I can hear Maxwell's voice. Sometimes I can make out what he is saying, and sometimes it is only the sound of him talking. Once, since he died, he has appeared in my dreams, as an old man who embraced me and said, "I'm glad I had you for a father." I am aware that Maxwell had grown fatigued by the effort of one day's following another — by having outlived his body, that is — and not much interested in going on without his wife, and that these are sufficient reasons to be grateful that his end was peaceful and without suffering. Even so, I am not resigned to his being gone. This is the contradiction at the heart of grief: there is no point at which I expect to say, I am happier than I was when he wasn't in the cemetery. We simply arrive eventually at a state of existence in which we are better able to bear the sadness. I keep a picture of Maxwell on my desk, and sometimes I forget it is there and raise my eyes from what I am doing and wonder how it is possible to feel so strongly about someone who isn't here anymore.

Six or eight years ago, when a woman I cared a great deal for died while she was still in her thirties, I thought for nearly a year that I saw her on the streets of the city. Out of the corner of my eye. Or her face reflected in a store window. Or her back as she turned into a doorway. Partly this was a result of how I felt about her, and her dying, which happened without my knowing of it and after a period when I hadn't seen much of her. Partly it was the result of there being other women who have her sleek figure, or red glasses like hers, or her short black hair, which she sometimes colored with henna. There are not that many old men on the streets in New York. Who move slowly, but with resolve, who might pause to take in the sight of schoolchildren coming toward them or to watch a young man break suddenly into a run to chase a bus. An old man with a coat on, though it's spring, and a hat. And maybe a scarf wrapped around his neck. A brown raincoat and a red scarf and a brown felt hat. So I don't have that experience. Some years ago, I was walking through Grand Central, on my way to the

Lexington Avenue subway, and I came to the top of the long stairs that lead to the turnstiles just as Maxwell placed a foot on the top step, as if he had come from the underworld or materialized from my unconscious because I had need of him. "How did this happen," I said. It was an occurrence to be grateful for, to rest my mind on — the way he was smiling, his radiance — even now. To meet your protector in a crowd, in the subway especially, where one expects nothing.

The day before Maxwell died I sat on his bed and, holding his hand, said what I had tried to keep in and instead it came out of me all at once: "How will I ever do without you?"

Before I could add "You don't have to answer that," he started to speak.

"You won't have to," he said, "because I won't ever leave you."

When my father gave up his job in the city, and he and my mother moved to their house in Wellfleet, my father began cultivating an oyster bed in the harbor. Every Christmas, he sent the Maxwells two dozen oysters. One year, Maxwell wrote to him:

"They were — there is no other word — exquisite. The best oysters I ever tasted. Twice in one year this has happened to me. Emmy's father served us a bottle of Chateau Margaux 1961 that had been given to him seven years ago on his eightieth birthday, and there is no better year or better wine for that year, and I realized that, alas, I have a palate for wine even though I don't know a bloody thing about it. And now the Wellfleet oysters. I also thought, as champagne glasses were raised to you, of what it meant trudging through the icy cold to get them for us, and who else would do it? The answer is nobody. There is no adequate way to thank you. It isn't even very sensible to try. I mean, you don't thank people for being your friend, you thank God for your good fortune in having them as a friend."